MATH POWER PACKS

Reproducible Homework Packets

Published by

Frank Schaffer Publications®

Columbus, Ohio

Frank Schaffer Publications®

Send all inquiries to:
Frank Schaffer Publications
8720 Orion Place
Columbus, Ohio 43240-2111

Math Power Packs—Grade 3

ISBN 0-7682-3493-X

2 3 4 5 6 7 8 9 10 GLO 12 11 10 09

Table of Contents

Dear Teacher,

We realize that extra homework practice is sometimes necessary for student success. *Math Power Packs* alleviate some of your heavy workload by providing ready-made homework packets right at your fingertips!

The packets in this book cover the six essential strands of mathematics—number and operations, measurement, algebra, geometry, data and probability, and problem solving—that are tested on standardized assessments. The packets were carefully crafted to meet national state standards and NCTM standards for school mathematics. To ensure that your students understand these important principles, a reproducible scoring rubric is included.

Each packet comes with a customizable cover letter to parents and ten activity sheets. All you have to do is fill in the appropriate information on the cover sheet for each packet, photocopy the reproducible pages, and send them home with your students. We recommend that you use these homework packets to reinforce the topics you are covering in the classroom. Send each packet home to give students further opportunities to practice skills, to help teach them responsibility, and to encourage independent work.

The home-school connection is an important one. To help strengthen and encourage rapport with your students' parents and guardians, we've included a blank calendar template. Use this to inform parents of homework due dates, upcoming quizzes and tests, and special events. There is an "additional notes to parents" section on each cover sheet that allows you to write specific notes and concerns home. You can also photocopy the math vocabulary sheet included in the book to send home so that parents fully understand the terms and concepts their children are practicing.

We trust that *Math Power Packs* will be a rewarding addition to your classroom. By utilizing the ready-made packets in this series, you are providing students with the extra learning power necessary for school success!

Sincerely,
Frank Schaffer Publications

Math Vocabulary List

acute triangle—a triangle with all angles measuring less than 90 degrees

addend—a number added to another number in an addition problem

area—the amount of surface within a certain space

associative property of addition—in an addition problem, the addends can be grouped in any way and the sum will remain the same

capacity—the amount that can be held in a certain space, often measured by cup, pint, quart, or gallon

commutative property of addition—in an addition problem, changing the position of the addends does not change the sum

congruent—having the same size and shape

dividend—a number to be divided by another number

divisor—a number by which another number is divided

edge—the place where two faces of a solid figure meet

equilateral triangle—a triangle with three equal sides

face—a flat surface of a solid figure

fact family—three numbers that are related and make a set of related math facts

factor—a number multiplied by another number

fraction—a part of a whole; a number written as one number divided by another

identity property of addition—the sum of 0 and any number is that number

identity property of multiplication—the product of 1 and any number is that number

inverse operations—two operations that have the opposite effect of one another

isosceles triangle—a triangle with two equal sides

line of symmetry—a line that divides a picture or shape into two equal halves

mean—the average of a group of numbers

median—the number in the middle when a group of numbers are put in order

mode—the number, or item, that you see most often in a set

obtuse triangle—a triangle with one angle measuring more than 90 degrees

odd—a number that cannot be divided evenly by 2

parallel—when two lines are in the same plane and never intersect

perimeter—the total distance around a shape

perpendicular—when two lines intersect and the angle between them is 90 degrees

polygon—a closed flat figure with three or more sides joined together

product—the result of two or more numbers being multiplied together

quotient—the answer to a division problem

range—the difference between the greatest number and the least number in a data set

right angle—an angle measuring 90 degrees

right triangle—a triangle with one angle measuring 90 degrees

sample—a smaller part of a group used for studying the characteristics of the whole group

scalene triangle—a triangle with three unequal sides

similar—the same shape but different size

sum—the result of adding two numbers

transformation—a change in the position, size, or shape of a figure

tree diagram—a diagram that shows the outcomes of a situation

vertex—the intersection of two sides of a figure; the point farthest from the base of a figure

volume—the amount of space inside a three-dimensional figure

zero property of multiplication—when you multiply a number by 0, the answer is always 0

Student's Name _____

Math Standards Scoring Rubric

1 = Does Not Meet **2 = Somewhat Meets** **3 = Meets** **4 = Somewhat Exceeds** **5 = Exceeds**

	Number and Operations
	Understands numbers, ways of representing numbers, relationships among numbers, and number systems.
	understands the place-value structure of the base-ten number system and can represent and compare whole numbers and decimals
	recognizes equivalent representations for the same number and generates them by decomposing and composing numbers
	develops understanding of fractions as parts of unit wholes, as parts of a collection, as locations on number lines, and as divisions of whole numbers
	uses models, benchmarks, and equivalent forms to judge the size of fractions
	recognizes and generates equivalent forms of commonly used fractions, decimals, and percents
	explores numbers less than 0 by extending the number line and through familiar applications
	describes classes of numbers according to characteristics, such as the nature of their factors
	Understands meanings of operations and how they relate to one another.
	understands various meanings of multiplication and division
	understands the effects of multiplying and dividing whole numbers
	identifies and uses relationships between operations, such as division as the inverse of multiplication, to solve problems
	understands and uses properties of operations, such as the distributivity of multiplication over addition
	Computes fluently and makes reasonable estimates.
	develops fluency with basic number combinations for multiplication and division and uses these combinations to mentally compute related problems, such as 30 x 50
	develops fluency in adding, subtracting, multiplying, and dividing whole numbers
	develops and uses strategies to estimate the results of whole-number computations and to judge the reasonableness of such results
	develops and uses strategies to estimate computations involving fractions and decimals in situations relevant to students' experience
	uses visual models, benchmarks, and equivalent forms to add and subtract commonly used fractions and decimals
	selects appropriate methods and tools for computing with whole numbers from among mental computation, estimation, calculators, and paper and pencil according to the context and nature of the computation and uses the selected method or tools
	Algebra
	Understands patterns, relations, and functions.
	describes, extends, and makes generalizations about geometric and numeric patterns
	represents and analyzes patterns and functions using words, tables, and graphs
	Represents and analyzes mathematical situations and structures using algebraic symbols.
	identifies such properties as commutativity, associativity, and distributivity and uses them to compute with whole numbers
	represents the idea of a variable as an unknown quantity using a letter or a symbol
	expresses mathematical relationships using equations
	Uses mathematical models to represent and understand quantitative relationships.
	models problem situations with objects and uses representations, such as graphs, tables, and equations, to draw conclusions
	Analyzes change in various contexts.
	investigates how a change in one variable relates to a change in a second variable
	identifies and describes situations with constant or varying rates of change and compares them
	Geometry
	Analyzes characteristics and properties of two- and three-dimensional geometric shapes and develops mathematical arguments about geometric relationships.
	identifies, compares, and analyzes attributes of two- and three-dimensional shapes and develops vocabulary to describe the attributes
	classifies two- and three-dimensional shapes according to their properties and develops definitions of classes of shapes, such as triangles and pyramids
	investigates, describes, and reasons about the results of subdividing, combining, and transforming shapes
	explores congruence and similarity
	makes and tests conjectures about geometric properties and relationships and develops logical arguments to justify conclusions

	Specifies locations and describes spatial relationships using coordinate geometry and other representational systems.
	describes location and movement using common language and geometric vocabulary
	makes and uses coordinate systems to specify locations and to describe paths
	finds the distance between points along horizontal and vertical lines of a coordinate system
	Applies transformations and uses symmetry to analyze mathematical situations.
	predicts and describes the results of sliding, flipping, and turning two-dimensional shapes
	describes a motion or a series of motions that will show that two shapes are congruent
	identifies and describes line and rotational symmetry in two- and three-dimensional shapes and designs
	Uses visualization, spatial reasoning, and geometric modeling to solve problems.
	builds and draws geometric objects
	creates and describes mental images of objects, patterns, and paths
	identifies and builds a three-dimensional object from two-dimensional representations of that object
	identifies and draws a two-dimensional representation of a three-dimensional object
	uses geometric models to solve problems in other areas of mathematics, such as number and measurement
	recognizes geometric ideas and relationships and applies them to other disciplines and to problems that arise in the classroom or in everyday life

Measurement

	Understands measurable attributes of objects and the units, systems, and processes of measurement.
	understands such attributes as length, area, weight, volume, and size of angle and selects the appropriate type of unit for measuring each attribute
	understands the need for measuring with standard units and becomes familiar with standard units in the customary and metric systems
	carries out simple unit conversions, such as from centimeters to meters, within a system of measurement
	understands that measurements are approximations and how differences in units affect precision
	explores what happens to measurements of a two-dimensional shape, such as its perimeter and area, when the shape is changed in some way
	Applies appropriate techniques, tools, and formulas to determine measurements.
	develops strategies for estimating the perimeters, areas, and volumes of irregular shapes
	selects and applies appropriate standard units and tools to measure length, area, volume, weight, time, temperature, and the size of angles
	selects and uses benchmarks to estimate measurements
	develops, understands, and uses formulas to find the area of rectangles and related triangles and parallelograms
	develops strategies to determine the surface areas and volumes of rectangular solids

Data Analysis and Probability

	Formulates questions that can be addressed with data and collects, organizes, and displays relevant data to answer them.
	designs investigations to address a question and considers how data-collection methods affect the nature of the data set
	collects data using observations, surveys, and experiments
	represents data using tables and graphs, such as line plots, bar graphs, and line graphs
	recognizes the differences in representing categorical and numerical data
	Selects and uses appropriate statistical methods to analyze data.
	describes the shape and important features of a set of data and compares related data sets with an emphasis on how the data are distributed
	uses measures of center, focusing on the median, and understands what each does and does not indicate about the data set
	compares different representations of the same data and evaluates how well each representation shows important aspects of the data
	Develops and evaluates inferences and predictions that are based on data.
	proposes and justifies conclusions and predictions that are based on data and designs studies to further investigate the conclusions or predictions
	Understands and applies basic concepts of probability.
	describes events as likely or unlikely and discusses the degree of likelihood using such words as *certain*, *equally likely*, and *impossible*
	predicts the probability of outcomes of simple experiments and tests the predictions
	understands that the measure of the likelihood of an event can be represented by a number from 0 to 1

Problem Solving

	builds new mathematical knowledge through problem solving
	solves problems that arise in mathematics and in other contexts
	applies and adapts a variety of appropriate strategies to solve problems
	monitors and reflects on the process of mathematical problem solving

What's Happening This Month

SUNDAY	MONDAY	TUESDAY	WEDNESDAY	THURSDAY	FRIDAY	SATURDAY

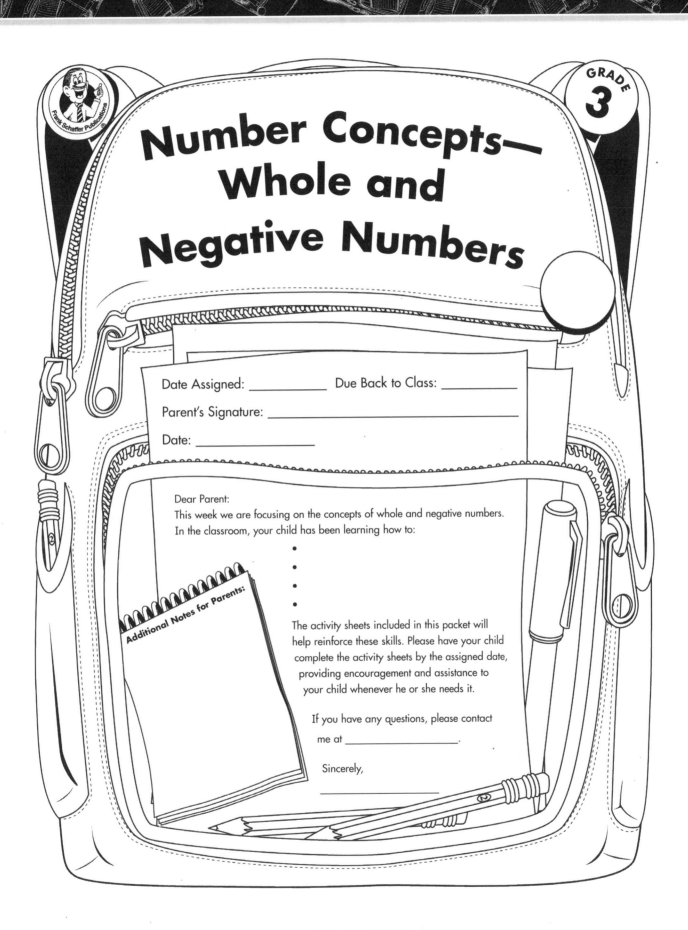

Number Concepts— Whole and Negative Numbers

GRADE 3

Date Assigned: _____ Due Back to Class: _____

Parent's Signature: _____

Date: _____

Additional Notes for Parents:

Dear Parent:

This week we are focusing on the concepts of whole and negative numbers. In the classroom, your child has been learning how to:

-
-
-

The activity sheets included in this packet will help reinforce these skills. Please have your child complete the activity sheets by the assigned date, providing encouragement and assistance to your child whenever he or she needs it.

If you have any questions, please contact me at _____.

Sincerely,

_____

Place Value

Use the clues to write a number in each box.

Clues

A. 3 in the hundreds place
B. 5 in the millions place
C. 6 in the thousands place
D. 4 in the ones place
E. 9 in the ten millions place
F. 8 in the tens place
G. 1 in the hundred thousands place
H. 2 in the hundred millions place
I. 0 in the ten thousands place

Millions			Thousands					
		,			,			

Write the numbers that make the sentences true.

1. In 2,648, the number _____ is in the tens place.

2. In 6,397, the number _____ is in the hundreds place.

3. In 6,873,251, the number _____ is in the hundred thousands place.

4. In 3,789,251, the number _____ is in the thousands place.

5. In 8,657,324, the number _____ is in the ones place.

6. In 8,158,760, the number _____ is in the millions place.

7. In 9,708,165, the number _____ is in the ten thousands place.

Name _____

Valuation

Write the number value of the underlined digit.

1. 3,6<u>8</u>1 = _____

2. <u>1</u>2,634 = _____

3. <u>4</u>7 = _____

4. 92,<u>4</u>10 = _____

5. 20<u>6</u> = _____

6. 3<u>2</u>5,172 = _____

7. <u>5</u>27,189 = _____

8. 6,0<u>1</u>7 = _____

9. <u>7</u>61 = _____

10. 1,8<u>2</u>3 = _____

11. 8<u>2</u>,610 = _____

12. 7,3<u>0</u>0 = _____

Name _____

Pull It Apart

Expanded Notation

$$2,507 = 2,000 + 500 + 7$$

Write the expanded form of each standard number.

1. 7,216 = _____

2. 34,928 = _____

3. 204,125 = _____

4. 831 = _____

5. 47,902 = _____

6. 616,000 = _____

7. 2,153 = _____

8. 90,306 = _____

Power Practice

Write each number in word form on another sheet of paper.

Math Power Packs: Reproducible Homework Packets *Grade 3*

Missing Information

Fill in the missing information. Sketch representational forms as follows:

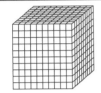 = 1,000   = 100   <tttttttt> = 10   ☐ = 1

1. representational form:
word form: two thousand, six hundred twelve
standard form:
expanded form:
circle one: even or odd

2. representational form:
word form:
standard form:
expanded form:
circle one: even or odd

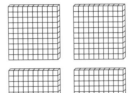

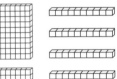

3. representational form:
word form:
standard form:
expanded form: 3,000 + 600 + 4
circle one: even or odd

4. representational form:
word form:
standard form: 4,037
expanded form:
circle one: even or odd

Think About It

How many tens? Example: 450 = 45 tens

1. 50 = _____ tens

2. 240 = _____ tens

3. 80 = _____ tens

4. 500 = _____ tens

5. 1,270 = _____ tens

6. 56,790 = _____ tens

How many hundreds? Example: 124,000 = 1,240 hundreds

7. 300 = _____ hundreds

8. 2,000 = _____ hundreds

9. 8,900 = _____ hundreds

10. 921,400 = _____ hundreds

11. 52,000 = _____ hundreds

12. 120,000 = _____ hundreds

How many thousands? Example: 46,000 = 46 thousands

13. 9,000 = _____ thousands

14. 78,000 = _____ thousands

15. 510,000 = _____ thousands

16. 672,000 = _____ thousands

17. 30,000 = _____ thousands

18. 102,000 = _____ thousands

How many . . . ?

19. 12,500 = _____ tens, _____ hundreds

20. 3,900 = _____ tens, _____ hundreds

21. 40,000 = _____ tens, _____ hundreds, _____ thousands

22. 619,000 = _____ tens, _____ hundreds, _____ thousands

Name _____

Comparisons

When numbers are compared, they can be greater than (>), less than (<), or equal (=). Write the correct symbol in the box between each set of numbers.

1. 345 ☐ 289

2. 67 ☐ 76

3. 1,290 ☐ 1,287

4. 5,388 ☐ 5,388

5. 724 ☐ 791

6. 32 ☐ 61

7. 562 ☐ 1,001

8. 463 ☐ 453

9. 29,284 ☐ 19,928

10. 610 ☐ 398

11. 125,902 ☐ 124,902

12. 89,352 ☐ 89,352

13. 20,671 ☐ 20,691

14. 39 ☐ 95

15. 521 ☐ 291

16. 8,152 ☐ 5,920

17. 72,891 ☐ 72,891

18. 648 ☐ 618

19. 92 ☐ 99

20. 125,627 ☐ 126,527

Name _____

The Next Number Is . . .

Intervals on number lines vary. Determine the next three numbers on each number line. Explain your answers.

1. ←|———|———|———|———|———|———|→
    56   66   76

      explanation:

2. ←|———|———|———|———|———|———|→
    1,244   1,242   1,240

      explanation:

3. ←|———|———|———|———|———|———|→
    225   250   275

      explanation:

4. ←|———|———|———|———|———|———|→
    630   740   8⁶0

      explanation:

5. ←|———|———|———|———|———|———|→
    99   89   79

      explanation:

Power Practice

Start with 50. Choose an interval. Make your own number line. Explain your number choices.

←|———|———|———|———|———|———|→
   50

50

Odd or Even?

> **Even** numbers can be divided equally into two groups.
> **Odd** numbers cannot. They are not divisible by 2.

1. Place any even digits in the top and bottom rows of each of these problems. Find the sums. What is true about the sum of two even numbers?

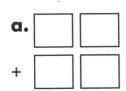   a.   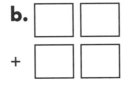   b.   c.

2. Place any odd digits in the top and bottom rows. Find the sums. What is true about the sum of two odd numbers?

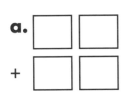   a.   b.   c.

3. Place even digits in the top rows. Place odd digits in the bottom rows. Find the sums. What is true about the sum of an even and an odd number?

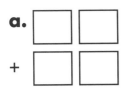   a.   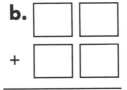   b.   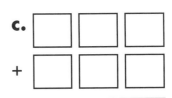   c.

Rounding

Round to the nearest ten.
Example: For 35 and up, round to 40.
For 34 and down, round to 30.

1_ _____	32 _____	58 _____
7_ _____	92 _____	82 _____
2_ _____	54 _____	66 _____

Round to the nearest hundred.
Example: For 350 and up, round to 400.
For 349 and down, round to 300.

92_ _____	662 _____	882 _____
458 _____	187 _____	363 _____
393 _____	527 _____	211 _____

Round to the nearest thousand.
Example: For 6,500 and up, round to 7,000.
For 6,499 and down, round to 6,000.

2,49_ _____	3,379 _____	4,289 _____
7,001 _____	8,821 _____	6,213 _____
5,111 _____	9,339 _____	2,985 _____

Negative Numbers

Use the number lines. Start at the given number and follow the directions. Write your answers using ⁻ and ⁺. Extend the number lines if necessary.

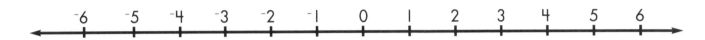

1. Start at ⁺6. Subtract 7, circle it. Where are you? _____

2. Start at ⁺4. Subtract 8, put a triangle around the number. Where are you? ____

3. Start at ⁺5. Subtract 7, put a box around the number. Where are you? _____

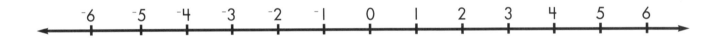

4. Start at ⁻6. Add 3, circle it. Where are you? _____

5. Start at ⁻5. Add 7, put a triangle around the number. Where are you? _____

6. Start at ⁻6. Add 5, put a box around the number. Where are you? _____

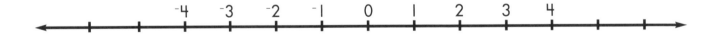

7. Start at ⁺1. Subtract 6, circle it. Where are you? _____

8. Start at ⁻3. Subtract 3, put a triangle around the number. Where are you? ____

9. Start at ⁻4. Add 9, put a box around the number. Where are you? _____

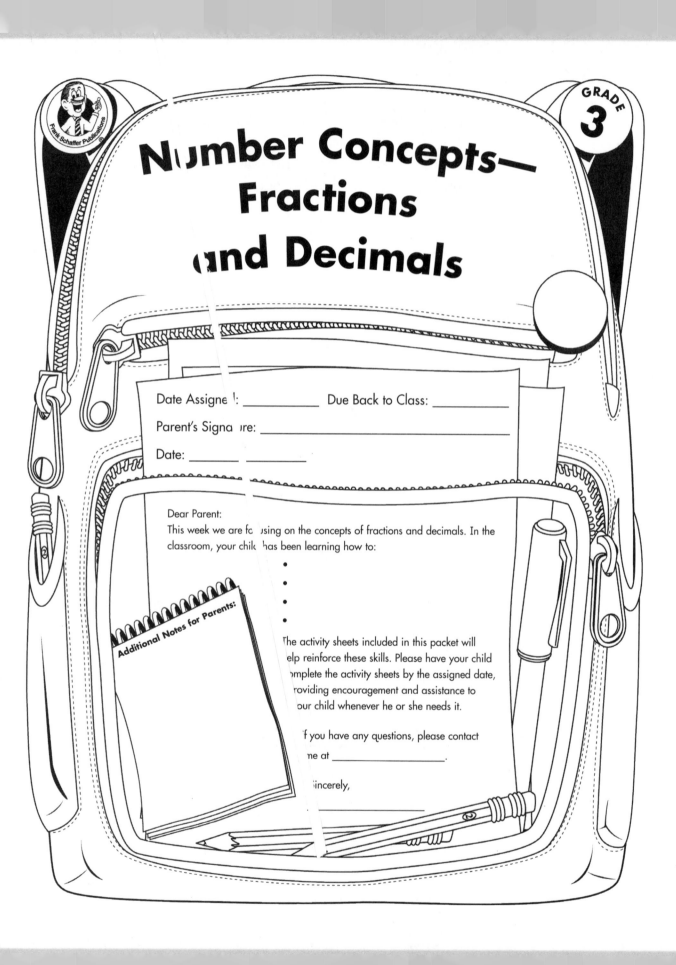

Number Concepts—Fractions and Decimals

GRADE 3

Date Assigned: _____ Due Back to Class: _____

Parent's Signature: _____

Date: _____

Additional Notes for Parents:

Dear Parent:

This week we are focusing on the concepts of fractions and decimals. In the classroom, your child has been learning how to:

-
-
-

The activity sheets included in this packet will help reinforce these skills. Please have your child complete the activity sheets by the assigned date, providing encouragement and assistance to your child whenever he or she needs it.

If you have any questions, please contact me at _____.

Sincerely,

_____

Fractions Among Things

Look at each group. Write the fraction for the following parts.

1. The total number in the group is _____.
   a. striped crabs _____
   b. shaded crabs _____
   c. white crabs _____
   d. striped crabs + white crabs _____
   e. white crabs + shaded crabs _____

2. The total number in the group is _____.
   a. white fish _____
   b. striped fish _____
   c. shaded fish _____
   d. striped fish + white fish _____
   e. white fish + shaded fish _____

3. The total number in the group is _____.
   a. striped _____
   b. dotted _____
   c. white _____
   d. shaded _____
   e. dotted + shaded + striped _____

4. The total number in the group is _____.
   a. striped seals _____
   b. white seals _____
   c. spotted seals + striped seals _____
   d. white seals + spotted seals _____
   e. striped seals + white seals + spotted seals _____

Fractions

 $\dfrac{1}{2}$ = $\dfrac{2}{4}$ $\dfrac{1}{2}$ and $\dfrac{2}{4}$ are equivalent fractions.

Fill in the missing numbers to make equivalent fractions.

1. $\dfrac{2}{4} = \dfrac{}{8}$

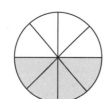

2. $\dfrac{1}{3} = \dfrac{}{}$

3. $\dfrac{1}{3} = \dfrac{}{}$

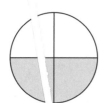

4. $\dfrac{3}{4} = \dfrac{}{}$

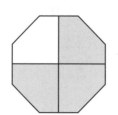

5. $\dfrac{1}{4} = \dfrac{}{12}$

6. $\dfrac{1}{2} = \dfrac{}{6}$

7. $\dfrac{1}{3} = \dfrac{}{12}$

8. $\dfrac{1}{3} = \dfrac{}{15}$

9. $\dfrac{2}{3} = \dfrac{}{6}$

10. $\dfrac{1}{2} = \dfrac{}{12}$

More Fraction Practice

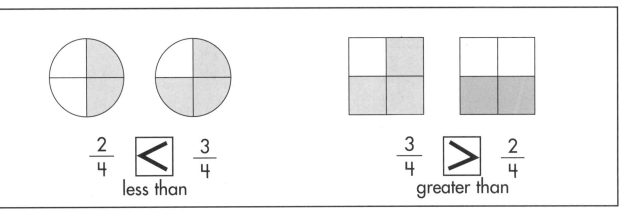

$$\frac{2}{4} \boxed{<} \frac{3}{4}$$
less than

$$\frac{3}{4} \boxed{>} \frac{2}{4}$$
greater than

Write < or > in each box.

1. $\frac{2}{3} \ \square \ \frac{1}{3}$

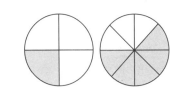

2. $\frac{1}{4} \ \square \ \frac{5}{8}$

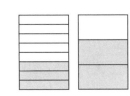

3. $\frac{3}{8} \ \square \ \frac{2}{3}$

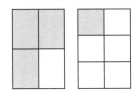

4. $\frac{3}{4} \ \square \ \frac{1}{6}$

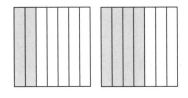

5. $\frac{2}{7} \ \square \ \frac{4}{7}$

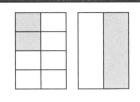

6. $\frac{2}{8} \ \square \ \frac{1}{2}$

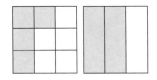

7. $\frac{4}{9} \ \square \ \frac{2}{3}$

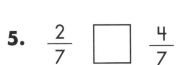

8. $\frac{3}{6} \ \square \ \frac{1}{4}$

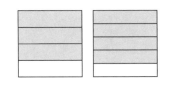

9. $\frac{3}{4} \ \square \ \frac{4}{5}$

Name _____

Get the Order

Sketch each fraction. Circle the sketch of the smallest fraction in the row. Use the diagrams to order the fractions from smallest to largest.

1. ○○○○○ ○○○○○ ○○○○○ ○○○○○
$\frac{1}{5}$ $\frac{3}{5}$ $\frac{2}{5}$ $\frac{4}{5}$ ___ ___ ___ ___

2. ○○○○   ○○○○   ○○○○   ○○○○
　　○○○○   ○○○○   ○○○○   ○○○○
$\frac{5}{8}$ $\frac{3}{8}$ $\frac{1}{8}$ $\frac{7}{8}$ ___ ___ ___ ___

3. ○○○   ○○○   ○○○   ○○○
　　○○○   ○○○   ○○○   ○○○
$\frac{6}{6}$ $\frac{3}{6}$ $\frac{5}{6}$ $\frac{2}{6}$ ___ ___ ___ ___

4. ○○○   ○○○   ○○○   ○○○
$\frac{3}{3}$ $\frac{1}{3}$ $\frac{0}{3}$ $\frac{2}{3}$ ___ ___ ___ ___

5. ○○○○○   ○○○○○   ○○○○○   ○○○○○
　　○○○○   ○○○○   ○○○○   ○○○○
$\frac{2}{9}$ $\frac{6}{9}$ $\frac{4}{9}$ $\frac{5}{9}$ ___ ___ ___ ___

6. ○○○○   ○○○○   ○○○○   ○○○○
$\frac{2}{4}$ $\frac{3}{4}$ $\frac{0}{4}$ $\frac{4}{4}$ ___ ___ ___ ___

Power Practice

What do you notice about ordering fractions with the same denominator?

Name _____

Order the Parts

Sketch each fraction. Circle the sketch of the smallest fraction in the row. Use the diagrams to order the fractions from smallest to largest.

1. ◯ $\frac{1}{3}$ ◯ $\frac{1}{6}$ ◯ $\frac{1}{2}$ ___ ___ ___

2. ◯ $\frac{1}{4}$ ◯ $\frac{1}{8}$ ◯ $\frac{1}{12}$ ___ ___ ___

3. ◯ $\frac{1}{2}$ ◯ $\frac{1}{12}$ ◯ $\frac{1}{5}$ ___ ___ ___

4. ◯ $\frac{1}{3}$ ◯ $\frac{1}{16}$ ◯ $\frac{1}{9}$ ___ ___ ___

5. ◯ $\frac{1}{4}$ ◯ $\frac{1}{1}$ ◯ $\frac{1}{2}$ ___ ___ ___

Tenths

Write the decimal that is equal to each word phrase. The first one has been done for you.

1. five tenths _0.5_

2. eight tenths _____

3. one tenth _____

4. five tenths _____

5. three and two tenths _____

6. eleven and nine tenths _____

7. nine hundred and six tenths _____

8. two tenths _____

9. forty-five and seven tenths _____

10. nine and eight tenths _____

11. eighteen and five tenths _____

12. four tenths _____

13. twenty-four and three tenths _____

14. one hundred twenty and three tenths _____

15. two hundred sixty-seven and eight tenths _____

16. thirty-one and one tenth _____

Power Practice

If the grid is worth one, shade the following decimals: 0.3, 0.9, 0.6, 0.2.

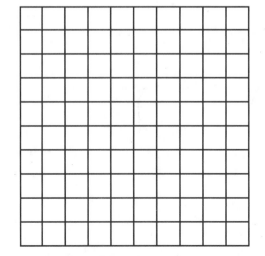

Name _____

Hundredths

Write the decimal that is equal to each word phrase.

1. nine hundredths _____   **2.** five hundredths _____

3. one hundredth _____   **4.** seven hundredths _____

5. sixteen hundredths _____   **6.** eighty-nine hundredths _____

7. forty-five hundredths _____   **8.** seven and two hundredths _____

9. five and four hundredths _____

10. sixteen and eleven hundredths _____

11. three hundred and three hundredths _____

12. seven hundred nine and four hundredths _____

13. six hundred twelve and seventy-one hundredths _____

14. twenty-four and one hundredth _____

15. thirty-three and two hundredths _____

Power Practice

If the grid is worth one, shade the
following decimals: 0.04, 0.09, 0.15, 0.81.

Picturing Decimals

Each grid is worth one. If the number is given, shade the decimal on the grid. If the shaded grid is given, write the number.

Example:

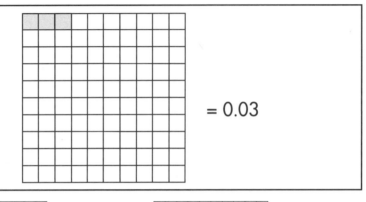

= 0.03

1. 0.5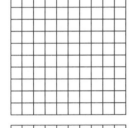

2. 0.06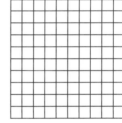

3. 0.61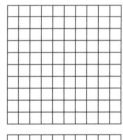

4. 0.34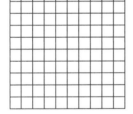

5. 0.7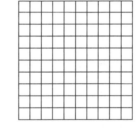

6. 0.04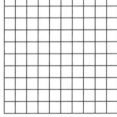

7. ____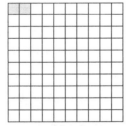

8. ____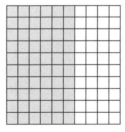

9. ____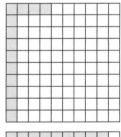

10. ____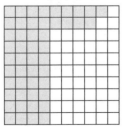

11. ____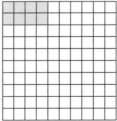

12. ____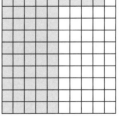

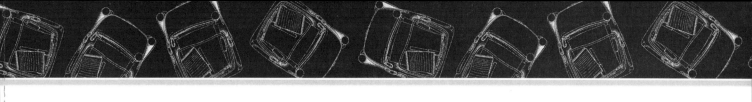

Dollars and Decimals

> A decimal point separates dollars from cents. Cents between $0.50 and $0.99 round up to the next dollar. Cents between $0.01 and $0.49 round down to the nearest dollar.

Keith's father gave him $360 to buy school clothes. He had to get everything he needed and stay within his budget. He needed 6 pairs of socks, 6 pairs of underwear, shoes, shorts, jeans, a track suit, and 3 shirts.

1. Keith chose these items. Round the cost of each item to the nearest dollar.

Cost	**Rounded Cost**
Socks: 6 pairs for $7.49	Socks: _____
Underwear: 6 pairs for $10.14	Underwear: _____
Shoes: $125.95	Shoes: _____
Shorts: $ 26.95	Shorts: _____
Jeans: $ 57.59	Jeans: _____
Track Suit: $68.75	Track Suit: _____
Shirts: $9.95, $15.97, $29.00	Shirts: _____

2. Use the rounded values to estimate the total price Keith will pay for the clothes. Show your work.

3. What is the difference between the estimated cost and his budget? Will there be money left over? Show your work.

Decimal Rounding

Round each number to the nearest tenth.

1. 0.341 _____ **2.** 0.69 _____ **3.** 0.225 _____

4. 1.634 _____ **5.** 67.409 _____ **6.** 21.062 _____

7. 3.55 _____ **8.** 10.13 _____ **9.** 92.98 _____

Round each number to the nearest hundredth.

10. 451.947 _____ **11.** 147.7232 _____ **12.** 5.198 _____

13. 17.1801 _____ **14.** 27.8456 _____ **15.** 36.6573 _____

16. 231.16208 _____ **17.** 446.996 _____ **18.** 52.577 _____

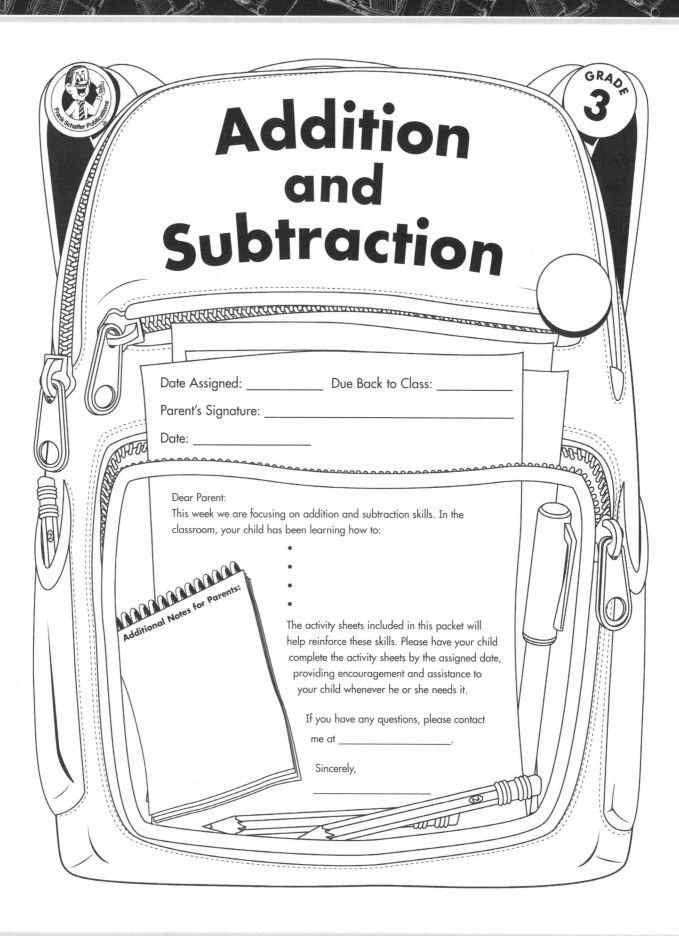

Addition and Subtraction

GRADE 3

Date Assigned: _____ Due Back to Class: _____

Parent's Signature: _____

Date: _____

Additional Notes for Parents:

Dear Parent:
This week we are focusing on addition and subtraction skills. In the classroom, your child has been learning how to:

- •
- •
- •

The activity sheets included in this packet will help reinforce these skills. Please have your child complete the activity sheets by the assigned date, providing encouragement and assistance to your child whenever he or she needs it.

If you have any questions, please contact me at _____.

Sincerely,

_____

Addition and Subtraction Families

The three numbers 4, 5, and 9 can be used to write two addition and two subtraction sentences:

$$4 + 5 = 9, 5 + 4 = 9$$
$$9 - 4 = 5, 9 - 5 = 4$$

This set of related number sentences is called a **fact family**.

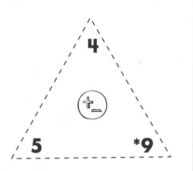

Place the three numbers in the corners of the triangle. Put a star by the largest number. Use the three numbers to write the four number sentences that make up the fact family.

1. 8, 9, 17

____ + ____ = ____

____ + ____ = ____

____ − ____ = ____

____ − ____ = ____

2. 15, 7, 8

____ + ____ = ____

____ + ____ = ____

____ − ____ = ____

____ − ____ = ____

3. 34, 15, 19

____ + ____ = ____

____ + ____ = ____

____ − ____ = ____

____ − ____ = ____

4. 23, 33, 56

____ + ____ = ____

____ + ____ = ____

____ − ____ = ____

____ − ____ = ____

Rebuilding the Pyramid

Add adjacent numbers together. Write their sum in the block above them. Continue adding until you reach the top block. Use your skills to fill in the missing blocks. Hint: Remember the relationship between adding and subtracting.

1.

| 6 | 8 | 3 | 9 | 5 |

2.

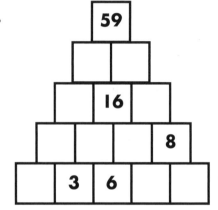

59, 16, 8, 3, 6

3.

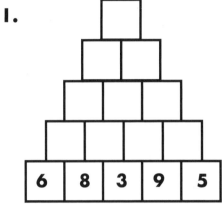

49, 26, 10, 6, 4

4.

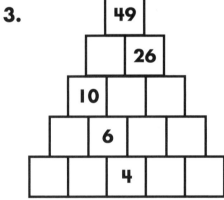

| 5 | 4 | 5 | 6 | 3 |

5.

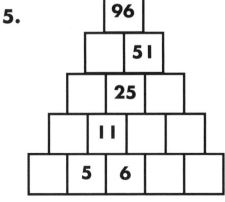

96, 51, 25, 11, 5, 6

6.

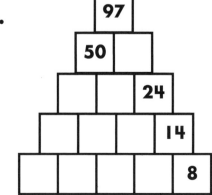

97, 50, 24, 14, 8

Name _____

Commutative Property of Addition

It's snack time! Give each animal its snacks. How many snacks in all?

1. Katy Kangaroo gets 7 bunches of grasses and 4 bunches of leaves.
How many bunches does Katy eat?
What if Katy eats the grasses first? $7 + 4 =$ _____
What if Katy eats the leaves first? $4 + 7 =$ _____

2. Freddie Frog gets 8 flies and 9 grasshoppers. How many insects does
Freddie eat?
What if Katy eats the flies first? $8 + 9 =$ _____
What if Freddie eats the grasshoppers first? $9 + 8 =$ _____

3. What do you notice? Does it matter in which order the animals eat? _____
Does it matter in which order you add the numbers? _____

You have discovered the
Commutative Property of Addition.
Changing the order of the addends
does not change the sum.

Addends
↓ ↓
$5 + 7 = 12$
↑
sum

Addends
↓ ↓
$7 + 5 = 12$
↑
sum

4. Color the following blocks in two ways to illustrate the commutative property.
Use an addition fact with the sum of 10.

Power Practice

Draw a number line. Show different ways to show the sum of $3 + 4 + 5$.

Associative Property of Addition

Do you know the order of operations? Do the work inside the parentheses ( ) first.

$10 - (3 \times 2)$	$10 - (3 \times 2)$
$10 - 6 = 4$	$7 \times 2 = 14$
Right	**Wrong**

The **Associative Property of Addition** says you can group the addends in any way. The sum is the same.

$$(3 + 7) + 2 = 3 + (7 + 2)$$
$$10 + 2 = 3 + 9$$
$$12 = 12$$

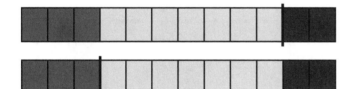

$(3 + 7) + 2$

$3 + (7 + 2)$

Write in the parentheses to show the associative property for addition. Fill in the numbers. Find the sums.

1. $4 + 5 + 9 \quad = \quad 4 + 5 + 9$

_____ = _____

_____ = _____

2. $11 + 4 + 16 \quad = \quad 11 + 4 + 16$

_____ = _____

_____ = _____

3. $5 + 8 + 12 \quad = \quad 5 + 8 + 12$

_____ = _____

_____ = _____

4. $20 + 38 + 10 = \quad 20 + 38 + 10$

_____ = _____

_____ = _____

Addition Practice

Help the ant get to the picnic. Complete the problems and shade each box that has a 9 in the answer.

836 + 90	536 + 248	952 + 8	362 + 47	486 + 293
789 526 + 214	2,846 + 6,478	932 + 365	374 + 299	956 874 + 65
4,768 + 2,894	38 456 + 3,894	4,507 + 2,743	404 + 289	1,843 + 6,752
639 + 77	587 342 + 679	5,379 1,865 + 2,348	450 + 145	594 + 278
29 875 + 2,341	387 29 + 5,614	462 379 + 248		

Three-Digit Models

Study each base-ten model. Circle the flats, rods, and units to be subtracted. Solve to find the difference.

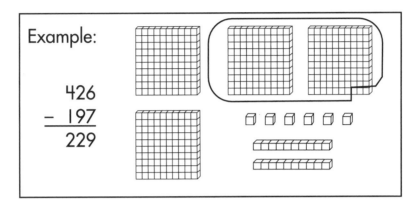

Example:

426
− 197
229

1.   743
     − 225

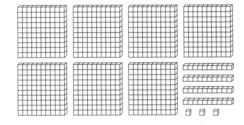

2.   503
     − 132

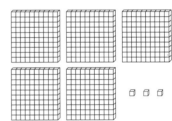

3.   621
     − 434

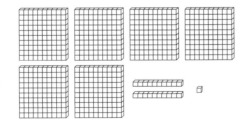

4.   427
     − 148

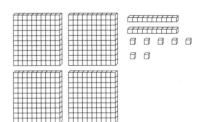

Make a base-ten model for each problem. Solve to find the difference.

5.   296
     − 198

6.   430
     − 271

Subtraction

Subtract ones.	Regroup. (1 hundred = 10 tens)	Subtract tens.	Subtract hundreds.
5 3 7 − 1 8 5 2	⁴ ¹ 5̸ 3 7 − 1 8 5 2	⁴ ¹ 5̸ 3 7 − 1 8 5 5 2	⁴ ¹ 5̸ 3 7 − 1 8 5 3 5 2

Subtract to find the answers.

1.
$$918$$
$$- \ 652$$

2.
$$738$$
$$- \ 284$$

3.
$$628$$
$$- \ 231$$

4.
$$437$$
$$- \ 175$$

5.
$$758$$
$$- \ 364$$

6.
$$878$$
$$- \ 690$$

7.
$$532$$
$$- \ 41$$

8.
$$425$$
$$- \ 362$$

9.
$$735$$
$$- \ 462$$

10.
$$989$$
$$- \ 296$$

11.
$$547$$
$$- \ 266$$

12.
$$827$$
$$- \ 382$$

Using Estimation

Round each problem to the nearest hundred. Find the estimated answer using your rounded numbers. Solve the original problem. Compare the actual and estimated answers.

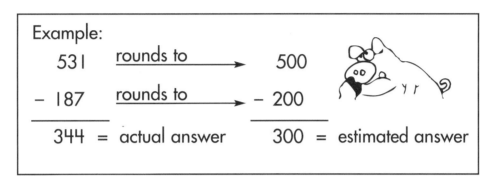

Example:

$$531 \xrightarrow{\text{rounds to}} 500$$

$$- 187 \xrightarrow{\text{rounds to}} - 200$$

$$344 = \text{actual answer} \qquad 300 = \text{estimated answer}$$

1.
$$\begin{array}{r} 346 \\ + \ 182 \\ \hline \end{array}$$

2.
$$\begin{array}{r} 763 \\ + \ 472 \\ \hline \end{array}$$

3.
$$\begin{array}{r} 586 \\ + \ 495 \\ \hline \end{array}$$

4.
$$\begin{array}{r} 217 \\ + \ 127 \\ \hline \end{array}$$

5.
$$\begin{array}{r} 467 \\ - \ 233 \\ \hline \end{array}$$

6.
$$\begin{array}{r} 931 \\ - \ 215 \\ \hline \end{array}$$

7.
$$\begin{array}{r} 546 \\ - \ 394 \\ \hline \end{array}$$

8.
$$\begin{array}{r} 321 \\ - \ 168 \\ \hline \end{array}$$

9.
$$\begin{array}{r} 461 \\ + \ 293 \\ \hline \end{array}$$

Just Three Digits

Use each set of three digits to write the largest possible number on the first line and the smallest possible number on the second line. Write and solve one addition and one subtraction problem with the two numbers.

2, 6, 4

largest = 642

smallest = 246

```
   246
+  642
------
   888
```

```
  5 3 1
  6/4/2
-  246
------
   396
```

1. 3, 9, 1

largest = _____ + _____ − _____

smallest = _____

2. 5, 2, 7

largest = _____ + _____ − _____

smallest = _____

3. 8, 1, 3

largest = _____ + _____ − _____

smallest = _____

4. 5, 9, 4

largest = _____ + _____ − _____

smallest = _____

5. 8, 7, 5

largest = _____ + _____ − _____

smallest = _____

6. 6, 1, 6

largest = _____ + _____ − _____

smallest = _____

Check With the Opposite

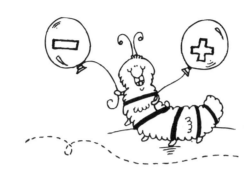

Solve each problem. Check the answers by using the opposite or inverse operation.

1.
```
  345
+ 275
```

2.
```
  197
+ 324
```

3.
```
  783
- 277
```

4.
```
  165
+ 149
```

5.
```
  903
- 364
```

6.
```
  255
- 119
```

7.
```
  712
- 458
```

8.
```
  263
+ 217
```

9.
```
  521
- 270
```

10.
```
  694
+ 745
```

11.
```
  842
- 163
```

12.
```
  317
+ 221
```

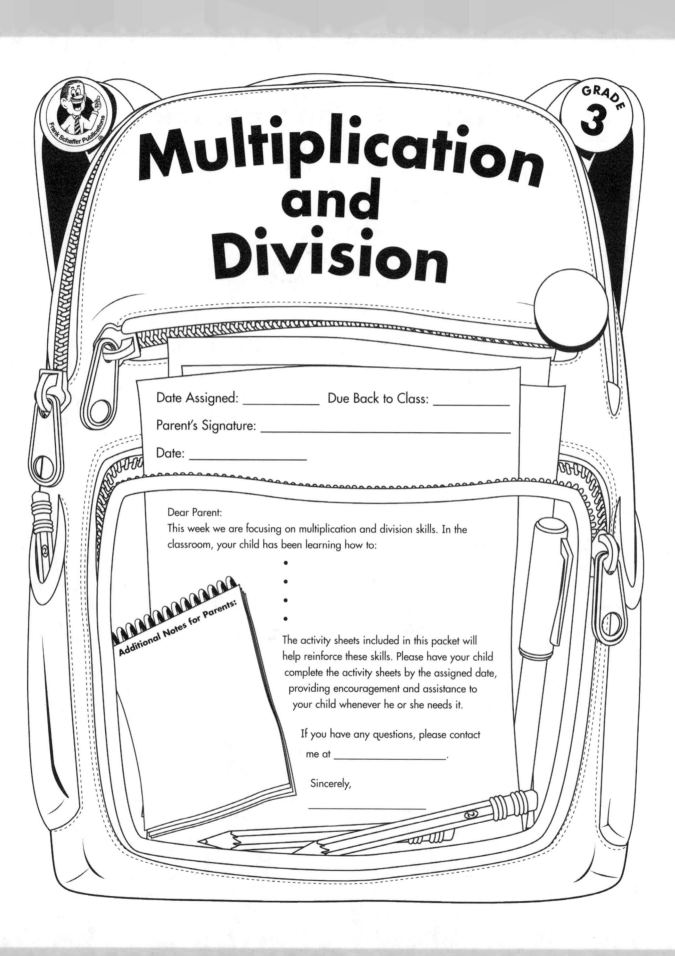

Multiplication and Division

GRADE 3

Date Assigned: _____ Due Back to Class: _____

Parent's Signature: _____

Date: _____

Additional Notes for Parents:

Dear Parent:

This week we are focusing on multiplication and division skills. In the classroom, your child has been learning how to:

- •
- •
- •
- •

The activity sheets included in this packet will help reinforce these skills. Please have your child complete the activity sheets by the assigned date, providing encouragement and assistance to your child whenever he or she needs it.

If you have any questions, please contact me at _____.

Sincerely,

_____

Groups

Multiplication requires counting groups with
an equal number of objects in each set.

•••• •••• •••• ••••

4 x 5 = 20
4 = number of groups or sets; this is the **factor**.
5 = the number of objects in each set; this is also a **factor**.
20 = the total number of objects; this is the **product**.

Make a sketch for each multiplication problem. Write the product.

1. 4 x 3 = _____   **2.** 8 x 5 = _____

3. 5 x 6 = _____   **4.** 2 x 9 = _____

5. 6 x 6 = _____   **6.** 7 x 4 = _____

7. 3 x 8 = _____   **8.** 1 x 5 = _____

9. 9 x 5 = _____   **10.** 4 x 4 = _____

11. 7 x 6 = _____   **12.** 3 x 9 = _____

The Garden on the Balcony

Courtney plants lots of flowers in her garden on the balcony. Look at each set of flowers. Then, write and solve the multiplication problem the flowers show.

1.

_____

2.

_____

3.

_____

4.

Multiplication

Multiply to find the answers.

1.
```
    6
  x 9
```

2.
```
    5
  x 3
```

3.
```
    8
  x 6
```

4.
```
    9
  x 2
```

5.
```
    7
  x 6
```

6.
```
    5
  x 6
```

7.
```
    8
  x 3
```

8.
```
    9
  x 8
```

9.
```
    4
  x 4
```

10.
```
    4
  x 6
```

11.
```
    8
  x 7
```

12.
```
    7
  x 4
```

13.
```
    8
  x 2
```

14.
```
    5
  x 5
```

15.
```
    7
  x 9
```

16.
```
    9
  x 3
```

Switching the Order

Find the answers. Notice that if you change the order of the factors, you have the same product.

1. 7 x 3 = _____

3 x 7 = _____

2. 6 x 5 = _____

5 x 6 = _____

3. 2 x 3 = _____

3 x 2 = _____

4. 4 x 6 = _____

6 x 4 = _____

5. 2 x 9 = _____

9 x 2 = _____

6. 8 x 4 = _____

4 x 8 = _____

7. 7 x 2 = _____

2 x 7 = _____

8. 3 x 6 = _____

6 x 3 = _____

9. 9 x 4 = _____

4 x 9 = _____

10. 8 x 3 = _____

3 x 8 = _____

11. 5 x 2 = _____

2 x 5 = _____

12. 9 x 3 = _____

3 x 9 = _____

Zero and One Properties

Multiplying by 1 (Identity Property): When you multiply a number by 1, the product is the number.

Multiplying by 0 (Zero Property): When you multiply a number by 0, the product is always 0.

Adding 0 (Identity Property): When you add 0 to a number, the sum is the number.

Follow the directions below to fill in the charts.

+	0	1	2	3	4
0					
1					
2					
3					
4					

x	0	1	2	3	4
0					
1					
2					
3					
4					

1. In the multiplication chart, fill in the row and column that show multiplying by 0. Write the products. What property is shown? _____

2. In the multiplication chart, fill in the row and column that show multiplying by 1. Write the products. What property is shown? _____

3. In the addition chart, fill in the row and column that show adding 0. Write the sums. What property is shown? _____

4. In the addition chart, fill in the row and column that show adding 1. Write the sums. Explain why this is NOT an identity or a zero property.

5. Fill in the remaining sums and products in the two tables.

Numbers in the Groups

Draw the sets. Then, write the division problem each drawing shows.

Example: Draw a total of 12 chocolate
chips in equal groups on 3 cookies.
<u>12</u> ÷ <u>3</u> = <u>4</u>

---

1. Draw a total of 14 buttons in equal groups on 2 coats.

_____ ÷ _____ = _____

2. Draw a total of 56 flies in equal groups on 7 windows.

_____ ÷ _____ = _____

3. Draw a total of 36 spots in equal groups on 9 ladybugs.

_____ ÷ _____ = _____

4. Draw a total of 35 eggs in equal groups in 5 nests.

_____ ÷ _____ = _____

5. Draw a total of 42 pretzels in equal groups in 7 bags.

_____ ÷ _____ = _____

6. Draw a total of 18 gems in equal groups on 6 rings.

_____ ÷ _____ = _____

Groups of Things

 Division requires equal distribution of objects into sets.

$12 \div 3 = 4$

12 = total number of objects; this is the **dividend**.
3 = the number of sets; this is the **divisor**.
4 = the number of objects in each set; this is the **quotient**.

Draw a sketch to show each division problem. Write the quotient.

1. $15 \div 5 =$ _____

2. $8 \div 4 =$ _____

3. $21 \div 7 =$ _____

4. $9 \div 3 =$ _____

5. $16 \div 4 =$ _____

6. $25 \div 5 =$ _____

7. $18 \div 9 =$ _____

8. $6 \div 2 =$ _____

Division

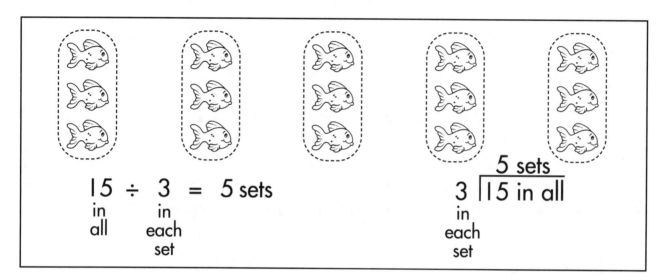

$$15 \div 3 = 5 \text{ sets}$$

in all / in each set

$$3\,\overline{)15 \text{ in all}} \quad 5 \text{ sets}$$

in each set

Divide to find the answers.

1. $8 \div 2 =$ _____ $2\,\overline{)8}$

2. $12 \div 4 =$ _____ $4\,\overline{)12}$

3. $21 \div 3 =$ _____ $3\,\overline{)21}$

4. $18 \div 3 =$ _____ $3\,\overline{)18}$

5. $20 \div 5 =$ _____ $5\,\overline{)20}$

6. $16 \div 4 =$ _____ $4\,\overline{)16}$

7. $14 \div 7 =$ _____ $7\,\overline{)14}$

8. $12 \div 2 =$ _____ $2\,\overline{)12}$

9. $18 \div 2 =$ _____ $2\,\overline{)18}$

10. $24 \div 6 =$ _____ $6\,\overline{)24}$

Related Operations

Addition and subtraction are related.

$3 + 7 = 10$ $10 - 7 = 3$

$7 + 3 = 10$ $10 - 3 = 7$

Multiplication and division are also related.

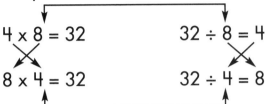

$4 \times 8 = 32$ $32 \div 8 = 4$

$8 \times 4 = 32$ $32 \div 4 = 8$

Three numbers that are related in one of these ways form a fact family.

Identify relationships in the following fact families.

1. Tell how the boxed facts are related. Describe what happens to the numbers.

   a. | $45 + 15 = 60$ | $60 - 15 = 45$ Description: _____

   | $15 + 45 = 60$ | $60 - 45 = 15$ _____

   b. | $9 \times 5 = 45$ $45 \div 5 = 9$ | Description: _____

   $5 \times 9 = 45$ $45 \div 9 = 5$ _____

   c. | $7 \times 6 = 42$ | $42 \div 6 = 7$ Description: _____

   | $6 \times 7 = 42$ | $42 \div 7 = 6$ _____

2. Write the missing fact in each set.

   a. $3 \times 7 = 21$ b. _____   c. $17 \times 1 = 17$ d. $0 + 29 = 29$

   $7 \times 3 = 21$ $50 + 40 = 90$ $1 \times 17 = 17$ $29 + 0 = 29$

   _____ $90 - 50 = 40$ $17 \div 1 = 17$ _____

   $21 \div 7 = 3$ $90 - 40 = 50$ _____ $29 - 0 = 29$

Multiplication and Division

x	1	2	3	4	5	6	7	8	9	10
1										
2										
3										
4										
5										
6										
7										
8										
9										
10										

Write the factors to complete the table. Use the table to solve the problems.

1.   8
   x 4

2.   5
   x 7

3.   48
   ÷ 8

4.   36
   ÷ 4

5.   3
   x 6

6.   42
   ÷ 7

7.   9
   x 5

8.   4
   x 7

9.   6
   x 9

10.   24
   ÷ 6

11.   49
   ÷ 7

12.   8
   x 3

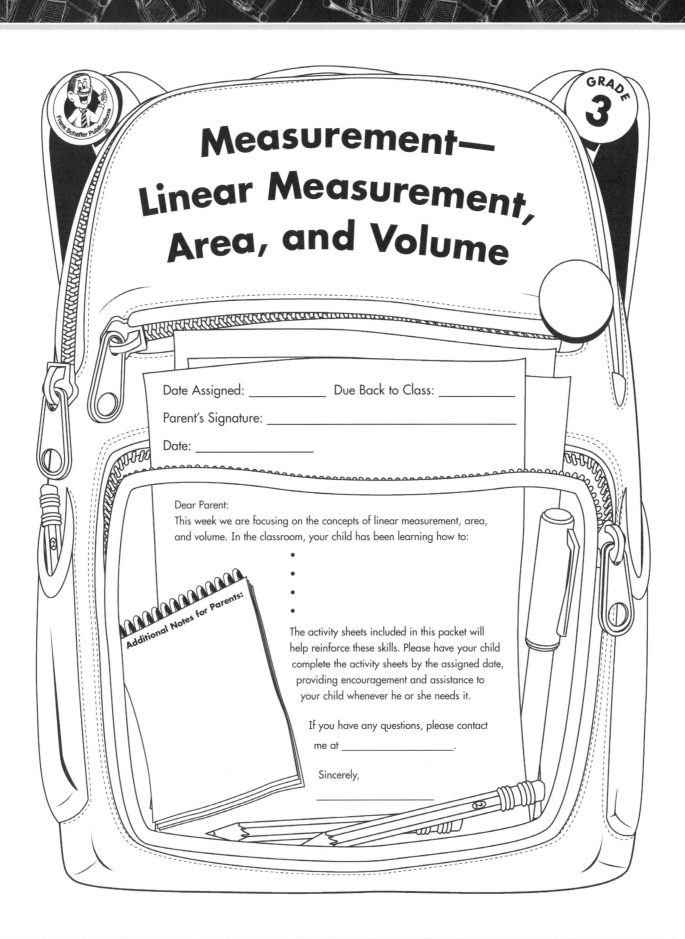

Measurement—
Linear Measurement, Area, and Volume

GRADE
3

Date Assigned: _____ Due Back to Class: _____

Parent's Signature: _____

Date: _____

Dear Parent:
This week we are focusing on the concepts of linear measurement, area, and volume. In the classroom, your child has been learning how to:

-
-
-
-

The activity sheets included in this packet will help reinforce these skills. Please have your child complete the activity sheets by the assigned date, providing encouragement and assistance to your child whenever he or she needs it.

If you have any questions, please contact me at _____.

Sincerely,

_____

Additional Notes for Parents:

Name _____

Measure Me

Use a ruler to measure the following lines in inches.

1. _____

2. _____

3. _____

4. _____

5. _____

Measure each line below to the nearest centimeter.

6. _____

7. _____

8. _____

9. _____

10. _____

Draw a line from the object to its approximate length.

                      1 centimeter

                      10 inches

                      18 centimeters

                      1.25 inches

   2 inches

Length Equations

Distance Measurements

12 inches = 1 foot
3 feet = 1 yard
36 inches = 1 yard

1 foot

3 feet = 36 inches

Use the measurements above to write equations for each problem. Then, write the answers.

1. How many inches are in 2 feet? _____ inches

2. How many inches long is a piece of ribbon that measures 1 foot, 7 inches? _____ inches

3. How many yards are in 30 feet? _____ yards

4. How many feet are in 14 yards? _____ feet

5. How many inches long is a fence that measures 2 yards, 20 inches? _____ inches

6. How many inches long is a rug that measures 1 yard, 2 feet? _____ inches

7. How many feet are in 37 yards, 1 foot? _____ feet

8. How many inches are in 2 yards, 2 feet, 2 inches? _____ inches

9. Write two questions using distance measures. One should be answered by a multiplication equation. The other should be answered by an addition equation.

Name _____

Metric Units of Length

The metric measuring system is based on multiples of 10. Below is a chart of metric conversions. Use the conversions to answer the questions.

1 centimeter (cm) = 10 millimeters (mm)
1 meter (m) = 100 centimeters (cm)
1 kilometer (km) = 1,000 meters (m)

1. Jodi measured her tomato plant. It is 34 centimeters. How many millimeters is this? _____

2. Meg has a plastic case that is 4 centimeters long. She found a shell that is 34 millimeters long. Will it fit in her case? _____

3. Kifa jumped 3 meters. How many centimeters is this? _____

4. Jordan's desk is 1 meter by 1 meter. He would like to put his science project inside his desk. The science project is on poster board that is 95 centimeters by 110 centimeters. Will it fit inside his desk without sticking out? _____

5. Anna is walking in a 5-kilometer charity event. How many meters will she walk by the time she reaches the finish line? _____

6. Jonathan is running in the 10,000-meter race. How many kilometers is the race? _____

Name _____

Perimeter

Perimeter is the distance around an area.

Find the perimeter of each figure below. Include the correct units in your answers.

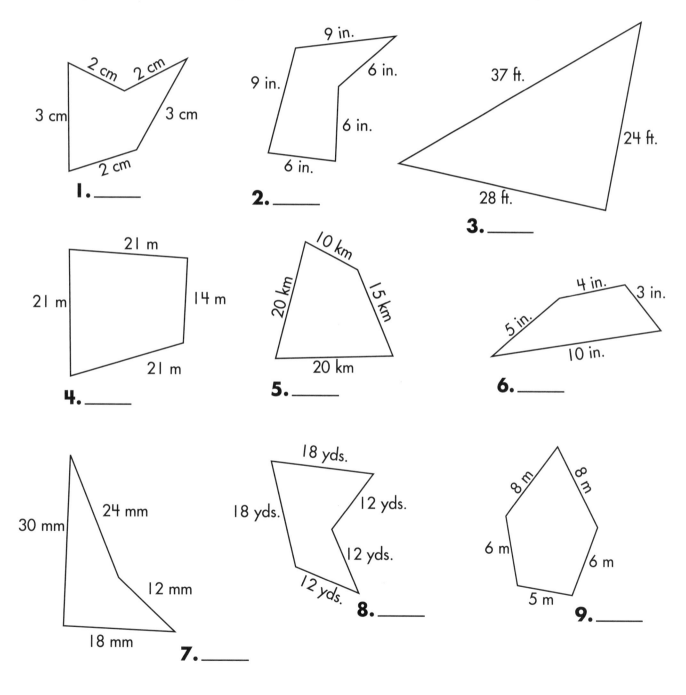

1. ____

2. ____

3. ____

4. ____

5. ____

6. ____

7. ____

8. ____

9. ____

Name _____

Area

Area is the amount of space inside a closed figure.

Find the area of each figure below by counting the square units. Each square measures 1 unit by 1 unit.

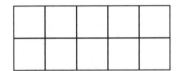

1. ____

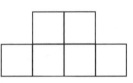

2. ____

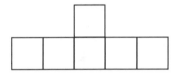

3. ____

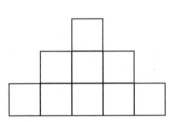

4. ____

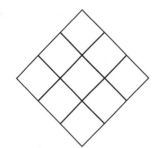

5. ____

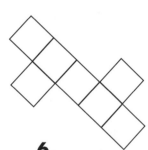

6. ____

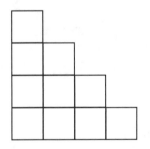

7. ____

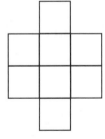

8. ____

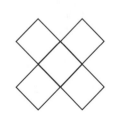

9. ____

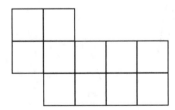

10. ____

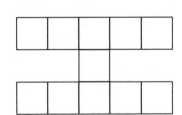

11. ____

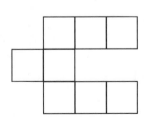

12. ____

Shaded and Un-Shaded

Find the shaded area of each grid.

1. 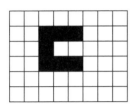 _____

2. 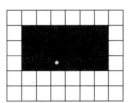 _____

3. 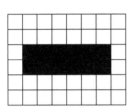 _____

4. 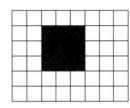 _____

Find the area of each shape.

5. 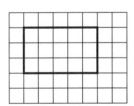 _____

6. 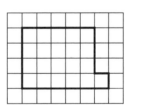 _____

7. 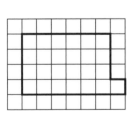 _____

8. 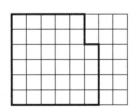 _____

Name _____

Perimeter and Area

Find the perimeter and area for each shape.

1.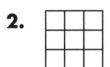

perimeter _____

area _____

2.

perimeter _____

area _____

3.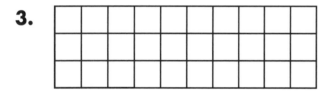

perimeter _____

area _____

4.

perimeter _____

area _____

5.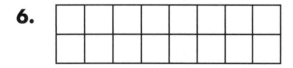

perimeter _____

area _____

6.

perimeter _____

area _____

Power Practice

 If the perimeter of a rectangle stays constant at 25 feet, what happens to the area as the shape becomes less long and thin and more like a square?

Shape Designs

Draw six shapes on the graph paper. Write the area and perimeter on each of your shapes. An example is provided below. Color your designs.

p = 14 units
a = 10 units^2

What Is Volume?

Volume is the amount of space inside a three-dimensional figure.

The volume of 1 cube is 1 cubic unit.

Find the number of cubes and the volume for each figure below.

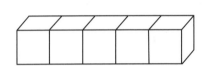

1. Number of cubes _____

    Volume = _____ cubic units

2. Number of cubes _____

    Volume = _____ cubic units

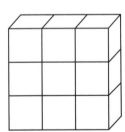

3. Number of cubes _____

    Volume = _____ cubic units

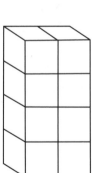

4. Number of cubes _____

    Volume = _____ cubic units

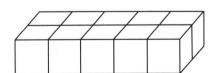

5. Number of cubes _____

    Volume = _____ cubic units

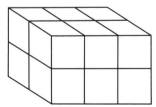

6. Number of cubes _____

    Volume = _____ cubic units

Name _____

Prism Volume

Find the volume of each prism.

1. 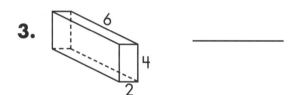 _____

2. 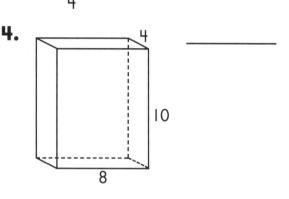 _____

3. _____

4. _____

5. _____

Use the information to find the volume of each rectangular prism described below.

6. length = 4, width = 2, height = 1 _____

7. length = 5, width = 4, height = 2 _____

8. length = 6, width = 3, height = 5 _____

9. length = 2, width = 4, height = 2 _____

10. length = 6, width = 6, height = 1 _____

Measurement—
Capacity, Mass, Time, Temperature, and Money

GRADE 3

Date Assigned: _____ Due Back to Class: _____

Parent's Signature: _____

Date: _____

Additional Notes for Parents:

Dear Parent:

This week we are focusing on the concepts of capacity, mass, time, temperature, and money. In the classroom, your child has been learning how to:

•

•

•

The activity sheets included in this packet will help reinforce these skills. Please have your child complete the activity sheets by the assigned date, providing encouragement and assistance to your child whenever he or she needs it.

If you have any questions, please contact me at _____.

Sincerely,

_____

Comparing Capacity

Look at the information in the box. Then, complete the equations.

2 cups = 1 pint	1 quart = 4 cups	1 gallon = 4 quarts

1. 3 pints = _____ cups

2. 2 quarts = _____ cups

3. 2 gallons = _____ quarts

4. 24 quarts = _____ gallons

5. 8 pints = _____ cups

6. 6 quarts = _____ cups

7. 12 cups = _____ pints

8. 5 quarts = _____ pints

9. 8 cups = _____ quarts

10. 6 gallons = _____ quarts

Name _____

Metric Units of Capacity

1 liter (L) = 1,000 milliliters (mL)
1 decaliter (daL) = 10 liters (L)
1 hectoliter (hL) = 100 liters (L)
1 kiloliter (kL) = 1,000 liters (L)

Find the following conversions.

1. 2,000 mL = _____ L

2. 6 daL = _____ L

3. 3 kL = _____ L

4. 1 kL = _____ daL

5. 4 hL = _____ daL

6. 500 mL = _____ L

7. 20 hL = _____ kL

8. 5 kL = _____ L

9. 70 hL = _____ kL

10. 42 daL = _____ L

11. 4,500 L = _____ kL

12. 9 daL = _____ L

Read the following problems and answer the questions.

13. Carl's pool holds 5,000 liters of water. How many kiloliters is this?

14. Elia has a 1-liter bottle of glue for refilling smaller bottles. The small bottle holds 200 milliliters. How many small bottles can she fill from the big one?

Selecting Appropriate Units

Circle the best unit of capacity for measuring the objects and containers below.

1.   mL   L   kL

2.   mL   L   kL

3.   mL   L   kL

4.   mL   L   kL

5.   mL   L   kL

6.   mL   L   kL

7.   mL   L   kL

8.   mL   L   kL

9.   mL   L   kL

10.   mL   L   kL

11.   mL   L   kL

12.   mL   L   kL

Name _____

Name _____

Ounces and Pounds

There are 12 ounces in 1 pound. Use this information to fill in each answer choice with either *ounces* or *pounds*.

1. A baseball might weigh about 6 _____.

2. Sara's dog loves to go running with her. Her dog weighs about 60 _____.

3. Maria's mom weighs about 140 _____.

4. Tina's shoelaces weigh about 1 _____.

5. Manolo's cell phone weighs about 10 _____.

6. Draw a picture of something that you think might weigh about 25 pounds.

7. Draw a picture of something that you think might weigh about 50 pounds.

8. Draw a picture of something that you think might weigh about 5 pounds.

         Math Power Packs: Reproducible Homework Packets Grade 3

Metric Units of Mass

1 gram (g) = 1,000 milligrams (mg) 1 kilogram (kg) = 1,000 grams (g) 1 decagram (dag) = 10 kilograms (kg) 1 hectogram (hg) = 100 kilograms (kg) 1 metric ton (t) = 1,000 kilograms (kg)

Find the following conversions.

1. 10 kg = _____ g

2. 1 hg = _____ dag

3. 2,000 g = _____ kg

4. 500 g = _____ kg

5. 70 hg = _____ t

6. 2 g = _____ mg

7. 3 t = _____ kg

8. 4,500 g = _____ kg

9. 30 kg = _____ dag

10. 6,000 mg = _____ g

11. 4 dag = _____ kg

12. 500 kg = _____ hg

Read the following problems and answer the questions.

13. Emilio has a bag of polished stones, each with a mass of 200 grams. How many stones are in the bag if the total mass equals 2 kilograms? _____

14. Tasha has a jar full of cookies with a mass of 175 grams. Each cookie weighs 5 grams. How many cookies are in the jar? _____

15. Kara has a collection of objects. Her plastic spider ring has a mass of 980 milligrams. A piece of quartz has a mass of 3 grams and a bag of buttons has a mass of 2,020 milligrams. What is the total mass of her collection in grams? _____

16. When Mark placed the green grapes on the scale, the mass was 200 grams short of 1 kilogram. He placed another 500 grams on the scale and decided to buy the whole bunch. How many grams in all did he purchase? _____

Matching Clocks

Draw lines to connect matching clocks.

1. 2:13   **a.**

2. 3:45   **b.**

3. 4:30   **c.**

4. 5:00   **d.**

5. 9:20   **e.**

6. 10:35   **f.**

7. 11:45   **g.**

8. 12:15   **h.**

9. 12:45   **i.**

10. 5:30   **j.**

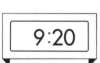

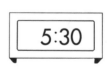

Power Practice

List the times above in order from earliest to latest, starting at 12:00.

Bathroom Countdown

First, read each clock. Then, read each sentence. Write the correct time on the second clock.

The time was....   **And now the time is....**

1.    It took José 5 minutes to brush his teeth.

2.    It took La'Votney 11 minutes to take a shower.

3.    It took Jill 15 minutes to wash her hair.

4.    It took Martina 4 minutes to put away the clean towels.

5. It took Grace 20 minutes to clean the floor.

Temperature

Temperature can be measured in two ways. In the U.S. customary system, temperature is measured in degrees Fahrenheit (°F). In the metric system, temperature is measured in degrees Celsius (°C). The chart below compares some commonly used temperatures for both systems. Use the chart to help you answer the questions.

	Fahrenheit	Celsius
water boils	212°	100°
body temperature	98.6°	37°
room temperature	70°	20°
water freezes	32°	0°

1. When the students first arrived at school in the morning, the classroom thermometer read 67°F. By recess, it read 73°F. What was the temperature change? _____

2. Mary is not feeling well. Her mother takes her temperature. The thermometer shows a temperature of 101°F. Should Mary stay home today? _____

3. The water temperature at the ocean was 69°F in the morning. By the end of the day, there was a temperature change of 6° and the temperature was colder. What was the temperature at the end of the day? _____

4. What is the temperature difference between 15°F and 43°F? _____

5. On a warm summer day in Toronto, Canada, the temperature at noon was 28°C. By late evening, the temperature had dropped to 19°C. What was the temperature change? _____

6. Josh and Daniel want to play ice hockey. The outdoor rink is only open if the temperature is below freezing. The thermometer reads 2°C. Will the rink be open today? _____

Show the Temperature

Fill in each thermometer with the temperature listed. Read each thermometer. On another sheet of paper, write one sentence describing the temperature and one sentence describing the clothes you might choose to wear based on the temperature.

1. 20°F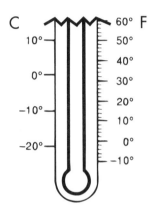

2. 40°C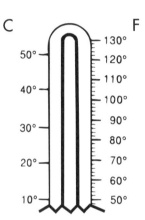

3. 32°F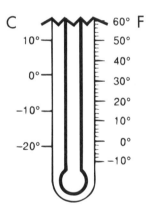

4. 101°F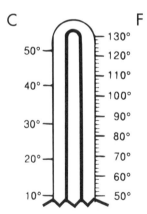

5. 0°C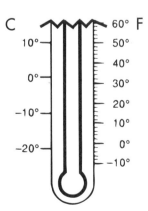

6. 50°F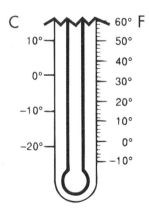

Using Money

Find the total of each set of coins and write it on the line. Complete the word problems.

1. _____

2. _____

3. _____

4. Meg has more than $1.25 but less than $1.50. Write the numbers of the sets of coins above that contain the amounts she could have.

5. Meg has 96¢. What is the greatest number she could have of the following coins:

   quarters _____   dimes _____   nickels _____

   What is the least number of pennies she could have? _____

6. Meg has 1 fifty-cent piece, 3 quarters, 2 dimes, and a penny. She wants to purchase a book for $2.00.

   How much does she have all together? _____

   How much more money does she need? _____

   What additional coins would bring her to the $2.00 total? _____

   Compare your coins with a friend. Talk about the coins chosen.

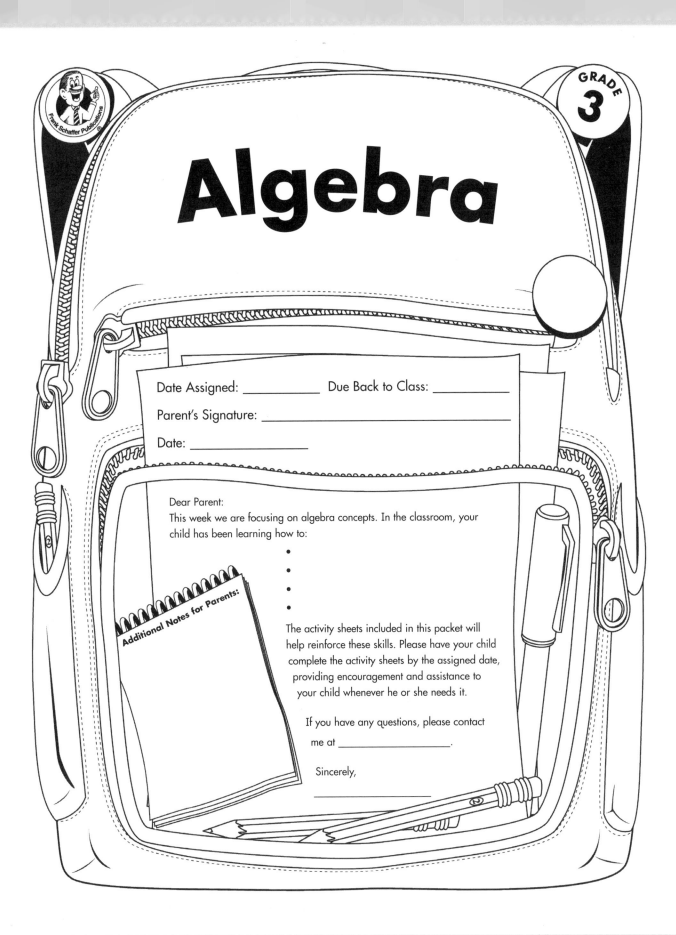

Algebra

GRADE
3

Date Assigned: _____ Due Back to Class: _____

Parent's Signature: _____

Date: _____

Dear Parent:

This week we are focusing on algebra concepts. In the classroom, your child has been learning how to:

- •
- •
- •

The activity sheets included in this packet will help reinforce these skills. Please have your child complete the activity sheets by the assigned date, providing encouragement and assistance to your child whenever he or she needs it.

If you have any questions, please contact me at _____.

Sincerely,

_____

Additional Notes for Parents:

Shapes in Line

Draw the shape that comes next in each row.

1. In this pattern, the shape changes.

2. In this pattern, the number of shapes change.

3. What changes in this pattern? _____

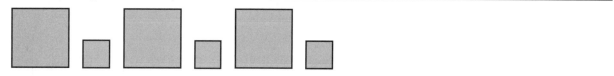

4. What changes in this pattern? _____

Power Practice

Draw a pattern in which the shape changes.
Draw a pattern in which the number of shapes changes.
Draw a pattern in which the size changes.
Draw a pattern in which the shading changes.

Name _____

Which Way?

A growing pattern has numbers that increase, such as 3, 6, 9, 12.
A decreasing pattern has numbers that decrease, such as 24, 22, 20, 18.

Write the missing numbers in each pattern. Circle **growing** or **decreasing**. Explain how you find your answers.

1. 3 7 11 ____ 19 23 **growing** **decreasing**

Explain. _____

2. 99 97 95 ____ 91 ____ **growing** **decreasing**

Explain. _____

3. 41 37 ____ ____ 25 21 **growing** **decreasing**

Explain. _____

4. ____ 128 138 148 ____ 168 **growing** **decreasing**

Explain. _____

5. 1 2 4 ____ 16 32 ____ 128 **growing** **decreasing**

Explain. _____

6. 500 401 302 203 ____ **growing** **decreasing**

Explain. _____

Power Practice

One of the patterns above is different from the others. Which one is different? Explain how it is different.

Number Patterns

Find the pattern in each row of numbers.
Continue the pattern to fill in the blanks.
Then, match the pattern to the correct rule.
The first one has been done for you.

Pattern	**Rule**
1, 3, 5, _7_, _9_, 11, 13	– 11
70, ____, 50, ____, ____, 20, 10	+ 12
1, 8, 15, 22, ____, ____, ____	+ 8
36, 33, 30, ____, ____, ____, ____	– 9
115, 100, 85, ____, ____, ____, ____	+ 2
64, 55, 46, ____, ____, ____, ____	– 10
17, 25, 33, ____, ____, ____, ____	– 3
96, ____, 84, 78, ____, ____, ____	– 15
88, ____, 66, ____, 44, ____, ____	– 6
12, 24, 36, ____, ____, ____, ____	+ 7

Two-Step Pattern Rules

Look for addition-subtraction patterns.

1. How does this pattern change from one number to the next? Fill in the boxes.

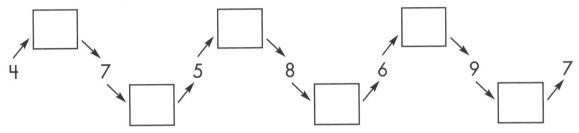

2. Describe the pattern rule in words. _____

You can describe the pattern using numbers and operations, such as + 3, then − 2.

3. Write the next three numbers in the pattern.

4   7   5   8   6   9   7   ____   ____   ____

4. Find the next pattern rules in the same way. Extend the patterns.

a. 10   17   13   20   16   23   19   ____   ____   ____

Rule: _____

b. 50   45   46   41   42   37   38   ____   ____   ____

Rule: _____

c. 44   39   45   40   46   41   ____   ____   ____

Rule: _____

Power Practice

Write your own pattern using an addition and a subtraction rule.

Follow the Rule

Follow the rule to complete each table.

1. These IN numbers are in order. Watch for the correct operation.

a. Rule: Add 2 **b.** Rule: Subtract 3 **c.** Rule: Multiply by 5 **d.** Rule: Divide by 2

IN	OUT
0	
1	
2	
3	

IN	OUT
20	
18	
16	
14	

IN	OUT
1	
3	
5	
7	

IN	OUT
2	
10	
18	
26	

2. The IN numbers do not have to be in order. They do not have to form a pattern.

a. Rule: Add 5 **b.** Rule: Subtract 4 **c.** Rule: Multiply by 2 **d.** Rule: Divide by 10

IN	OUT
12	
15	
21	
57	

IN	OUT
14	
8	
10	
43	

IN	OUT
0	
9	
11	
50	

IN	OUT
90	
10	
30	
60	

3. Fill in either the IN number or the OUT number.

a. Rule: Add 12

IN	0	5			
OUT			22	13	

b. Rule: Multiply by 6

IN		4		9	
OUT	12		42		

Guess the Rule

Guess the rule for each table. Write the rule and complete the table.

1.

IN	0	1	2	3	4
OUT			9	10	

Rule: _____

2.

IN	27	24	21	18	15
OUT	9			6	

Rule: _____

3.

IN	19	24	33	9	
OUT	10			0	45

Rule: _____

4.

IN			33	58	100
OUT	1	21	12	37	

Rule: _____

5.

IN	36	44		16	
OUT		11	6	4	2

Rule: _____

6.

IN	4	3	0	9	5
OUT		21	0		35

Rule: _____

7.

IN	7	9	10	5	
OUT		81		45	27

Rule: _____

8.

IN	10	11			18
OUT		22	46	18	29

Rule: _____

Shape Values

Shapes and letters can stand for missing numbers.

$n + 7 = 13 \qquad n = 6$

$\blacksquare + 7 = 13 \qquad \blacksquare = 6$

Use shapes to stand for unknown numbers.

1. Find the value of each shape.

a. $8 \times \blacksquare = 56$

$\blacksquare = $ _____

b. $7 + \blacktriangle = 19$

$\blacktriangle = $ _____

c. $16 \div \bullet = 8$

$\bullet = $ _____

d. $4 \times \blacktriangle = 36$

$\blacktriangle = $ _____

e. $35 - \text{⬡} = 5$

$\text{⬡} = $ _____

f. $\blacktriangledown \times 9 = 72$

$\blacktriangledown = $ _____

g. $\blacksquare + 15 = 41$

$\blacksquare = $ _____

h. $212 - \text{⬠} = 199$

$\text{⬠} = $ _____

i. $\bullet \div 7 = 9$

$\bullet = $ _____

2. Use the two numbers to write four related addition and subtraction facts. What number can the $\blacksquare$ represent? _____ 12, $\blacksquare$, 5

3. What other number could $\blacksquare$ represent? _____ Use the same two numbers to write four different addition-subtraction facts.

4. Use the two numbers to write four related multiplication and division facts. What number could the $\bullet$ represent? _____ 9, 5, $\bullet$

5. Can you write another fact family with the numbers in problem 4? Explain.

Name _____

Number Letters

Each problem has a letter in place of a number. Use what you know about addition and subtraction to determine the missing number.

1. $3 + m = 29$

m = _____

2. $17 + 7 = a + 8$

a = _____

3. $33 + 17 = s - 8$

s = _____

4. $55 - 17 = t$

t = _____

5. $u + 3 = 18 + 16$

u = _____

6. $23 + 15 = 19 + o$

o = _____

7. $b + 23 = 43$

b = _____

8. $f = 27 + 46$

f = _____

9. $75 - e = 30 + 5$

e = _____

10. $2 + d = 49 + 5$

d = _____

11. $24 = r + 1$

r = _____

12. $l = 31 - 9$

l = _____

13. $47 = n + 5$

n = _____

14. $7 + g = 14 + 11$

g = _____

15. $c = 21 - 4$

c = _____

Use the answers from the problems to fill in the letters below and reveal a message.

___ ___ ___ ___ ___ ___   ___ ___ ___ ___ ___ ___ ___
42 31 26 20 40 23   22 40 38 38 40 23 58

___ ___ ___ ___ ,   ___ ___ ___ ___ ___   ___ ___ !
52 19 42 38   58 17 16 23 40   26 40

Graphing Lines

Ordered pairs locate points on a grid. Use (x, y) where x tells how many units to count to the right, and y tells how many units to count up.

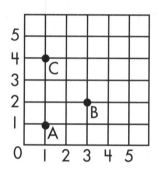

Example: Point A is at (1, 1). Point B is at (3, 2).
Point C is at (1, 4).

Graph the points. Tell what you find.

1. A (7, 5)
B (7, 9)
C (3, 9)
D (3, 5)
Connect the points.
What have you made?

2. Q (3, 1)
R (8, 9)
P (2, 5)
Connect the points.
What have you made?

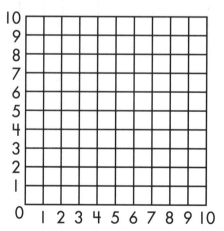

Power Practice

How many points do you need to draw a line on the grid?

Name the Vertices

Name the ordered pair for each vertex of the shapes shown.

1.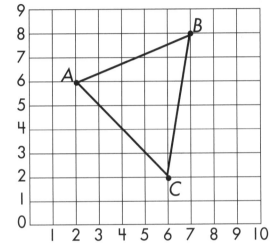

A_____ B_____ C_____

2.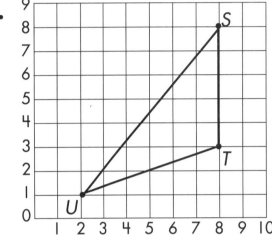

S_____ T_____ U_____

3.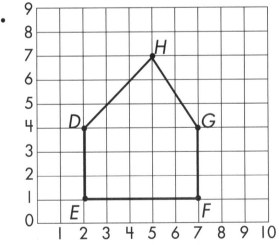

D_____ E_____ F_____

G_____ H_____

4.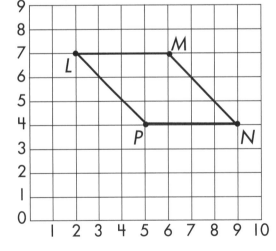

L_____ M_____

N_____ P_____

Power Practice

Describe how you found the ordered pair for vertex P.

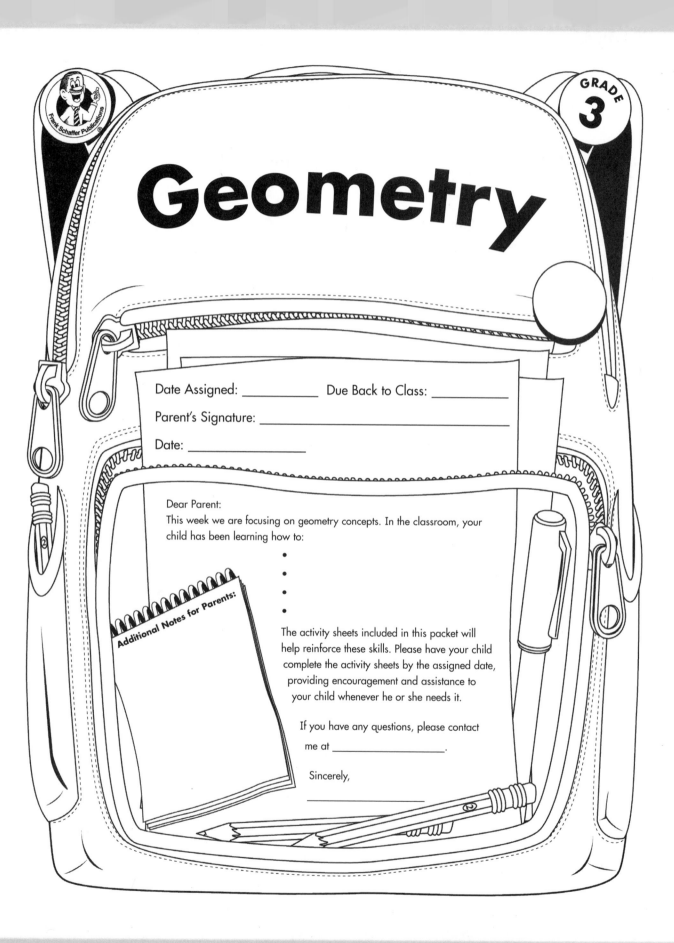

Geometry

GRADE 3

Date Assigned: _____ Due Back to Class: _____

Parent's Signature: _____

Date: _____

Additional Notes for Parents:

Dear Parent:

This week we are focusing on geometry concepts. In the classroom, your child has been learning how to:

-
-
-
-

The activity sheets included in this packet will help reinforce these skills. Please have your child complete the activity sheets by the assigned date, providing encouragement and assistance to your child whenever he or she needs it.

If you have any questions, please contact me at _____.

Sincerely,

_____

Parallel and Perpendicular Lines

Lines that intersect each other to form right angles are **perpendicular lines**.

Lines that do not intersect each other are **parallel lines**.

Is each set of lines parallel, perpendicular, or neither? Circle the correct answer choice.

1.
parallel
perpendicular
neither

2.
parallel
perpendicular
neither

3.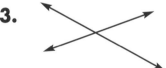
parallel
perpendicular
neither

4.
parallel
perpendicular
neither

5.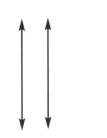
parallel
perpendicular
neither

6.
parallel
perpendicular
neither

Power Practice

Do the sides of a door model parallel or perpendicular lines? Does the corner of this piece of paper model parallel or perpendicular lines?

Name _____

The Right Angle

This ∟ is a **right angle**. For each angle below, write >, <, or = to compare it to a right angle. The greater than symbol means it is more than 90°. The less than symbol means it is less than 90°. The equals symbol means it is equal to 90°.

1.

2.

3.

4.

5.

6.

7.

8.

Drawing Lines of Symmetry

A **line of symmetry** is a line that divides a picture or shape into two equal halves. Each half is a mirror image of the other half. A line of symmetry can be vertical, horizontal, or diagonal.

A square has 4 lines of symmetry.

Draw the line or lines of symmetry for each shape.

1.

2.

3.

4.

5.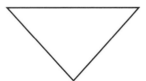

6.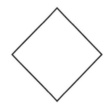

Power Practice

 Draw a shape that does not have a line of symmetry.

Match the Transformation

Circle the picture that shows the named transformation.

1. Flip

2. Slide

3. Turn

4. Turn

5. Slide

Congruent or Similar?

Congruent—the same size and shape.	**Similar**—the same shape, but different sizes.

Classify each pair below as **congruent**, **similar**, or **neither**.

1.

_____

2.

_____

3.

_____

4.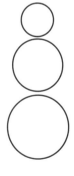

_____

5.

_____

6.

_____

Look at each shape below. Draw a shape that is **similar**.

7.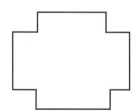

8.

Types of Triangles

Right Triangle—One of the angles measures 90 degrees (an L-shaped angle).

Acute Triangle—All angles in the triangle measure less than 90 degrees.

Obtuse Triangle—One of the angles measures more than 90 degrees.

Isosceles Triangle—Two of the sides are equal.

Equilateral Triangle—All three sides are equal.

Scalene Triangle—No sides are equal.

Follow the instructions for each type of triangle. Remember, triangles can be more than one type.

- Color all the **right** triangles blue.
- Color all the **acute** triangles red.
- Color all the **obtuse** triangles green.
- Circle all the **isosceles** triangles.
- Put a box around all the **equilateral** triangles.
- Put a line beneath all the **scalene** triangles.

Name _____

Types of Polygons

The word **polygon** means "many sides." Polygons are grouped into different categories based on their number of sides and angles, as shown in the chart. A shape with any curved sides is not a polygon.	Polygon Name	Number of Sides and Angles
	a. Triangle	3
	b. Quadrilateral	4
	c. Pentagon	5
	d. Hexagon	6
	e. Heptagon	7
	f. Octagon	8
	g. Not a polygon	

Put the letter of the polygon name that matches each shape on the blank next to the shape. Or, if the shape is not a polygon, put the letter g on the blank. The polygon names may be used more than once.

___ 1. ⬡   ___ 2. ⬠   ___ 3. △

___ 4. ▱   ___ 5. ⬡   ___ 6. ▱

___ 7. ⋈   ___ 8. D

___ 9. ⬡   ___ 10. ○   

Name _____

Cones, Cylinders, and Spheres

The **vertex** of a three-dimensional shape is the place where it comes to a point.

Cylinder   **Cone**   **Sphere**

Fill in the blanks with the shape (**cone**, **cylinder**, or **sphere**) that makes each sentence true.

1. A _____ has no vertex.

2. A _____ can roll in a straight line.

3. A _____ will look like a rectangle if it is unrolled.

4. A _____ has one vertex.

5. A _____ has 2 circular bases.

6. A _____ has 1 circular base.

7. A _____ can roll, but not in a straight line.

8. A _____ has no flat face.

Next to each object, write the name of the 3-dimensional shape it most resembles.

9. _____   **10.** _____   **11.**  _____

How Many Faces and Edges?

A **face** is a flat surface of a solid figure.
The place where two faces of a solid figure meet is an **edge**.

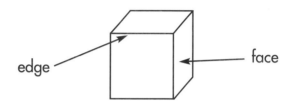

edge   face

Fill in the blanks.

1. number of faces _____ number of edges _____

2. number of faces _____ number of edges _____

3. number of faces _____ number of edges _____

4. number of faces _____ number of edges _____

Name _____

What Will I Make?

Draw a line to match the description with the correct shape.

1. 6 square faces

2. 1 square, 4 triangles

3. 4 sides, 2 obtuse angles, 2 acute angles

4. 4 sides of equal length

5. 1 right angle, 2 acute angles

6. 8 angles and 8 sides

7. 1 rectangle, 2 circular bases

8. 3 acute angles

9. 2 triangles, 3 rectangles

10. 1 circular base

11. 1 obtuse angle, 2 acute angles

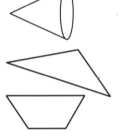

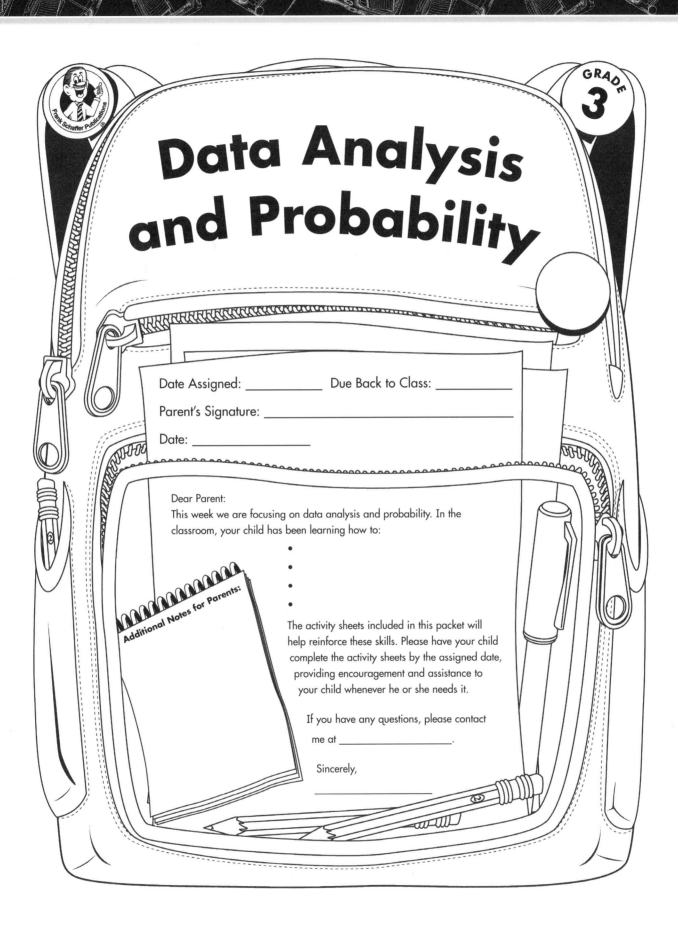

Data Analysis and Probability

Frank Schaffer Publications®

GRADE 3

Date Assigned: _____ Due Back to Class: _____

Parent's Signature: _____

Date: _____

Additional Notes for Parents:

Dear Parent:
This week we are focusing on data analysis and probability. In the classroom, your child has been learning how to:

- •
- •
- •
- •

The activity sheets included in this packet will help reinforce these skills. Please have your child complete the activity sheets by the assigned date, providing encouragement and assistance to your child whenever he or she needs it.

If you have any questions, please contact me at _____.

Sincerely,

_____

Name _____

Make a Bar Graph

Make a bar graph using the data in the tally chart.
Be sure to include a scale, labels, and a title.

Favorite Type of Music		
Type of Music	**Tally**	**Number**
Rock and Roll	卌 ||||	9
Country	卌 |	6
Oldies	||||	4
Rap	卌 ||	7

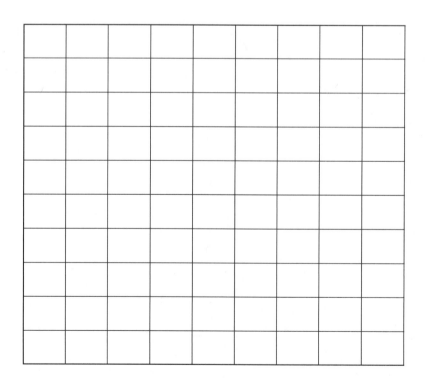

Circle Graph

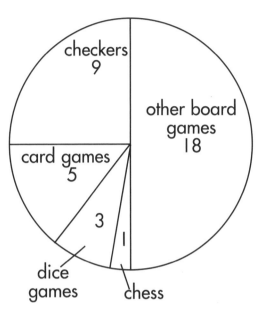

A **circle graph** represents data by dividing a circle into parts. Students in Sari's class had a special game day. Sari went around the room and noted how many students were playing at each game station at a given time. She recorded her findings in a circle graph.

Use the circle graph to answer the questions.

1. What is the total number of students in Sari's class that played on game day?_____

2. One game station was very popular, with half of the students playing there. Which station was it? _____

3. Which game station had the fewest players? _____

4. If Sari combined the dice games, card games, and chess stations, would that new group be larger, smaller, or the same size as the checkers group? _____

5. Half as many students played checkers as played at which game station? _____

6. Sari's teacher needs to plan for next year's game day. Which game should she consider taking out? _____

Which two games should she be sure to include? _____

Line Graph

A **line graph** can show change over time.

Carla's mother made this chart of Carla's height since she was 2 years old. Finish the graph and answer the questions.

Carla's Growth

Age	Height (in inches)
2	34
4	39
6	44
8	52
10	54
12	60

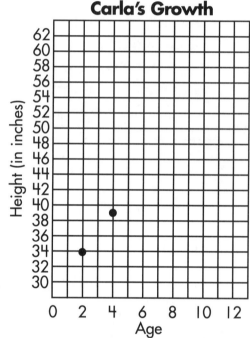

Carla's Growth

1. What do the points on the graph tell you?

2. Explain how you know where to place the points for how tall Carla was at 6 years old.

3. Finish the graph to show how tall Carla was at 6, 8, 10, and 12 years old. Highlight the points by making dark dots.

4. Connect the dots. Begin at the point for 2 years old at 34 inches and connect each point to the next one.

   a. You can estimate values between the points. How tall do you think Carla was at 9 years old?

   b. How tall do you think Carla was at 5 years old?

   c. Does the graph show a rate of change that is constant or uneven?

   d. Can you predict how tall Carla will be at 14 years old? _____ Explain.

Statistics

Statistics are used to give an overall score for a set of data.
Here are 3 commonly used statistics.

Mean:
average

Median:
middle

Mode:
number that occurs most often

1. Sam is 12 years old. His brothers and sisters are 2, 5, 9, and 16 years old.

   a. What is the **mean** age of the children in Sam's family?

      Sum: 2 + 5 + 9 + 12 + 16 = _____

      Mean: _____ ÷ 5 children = _____

   b. What is the **median** age of children in Sam's family?

      Ages in order: 2, 5, 9, 12, 16

      Put a slash through the smallest and largest number. Then, put a mark
through the next lowest and highest numbers. Continue to cross out
numbers, working toward the center. Circle the middle number.

      Median = _____

   c. Does this group of data have a **mode**? Explain.

2. Cindy ran 3 miles on Monday, 5 miles on Tuesday, 7 miles on Wednesday,
4 miles on Thursday, and 5 miles on Friday.

   a. What is the **mean** number of miles? Show your work.

   b. What is the **median** number of miles? Show your work.

   c. What is the **mode** number of miles?

The Range

The **range** is the difference between the greatest number and the least number in a data set.

To find the range, subtract the least data value from the greatest data value.

Find the range of each set of numbers.

1. 2, 4, 5, 6, 8

_____

2. 3, 3, 5, 7, 9

_____

3. 4, 5, 6, 7, 9, 10, 12

_____

4. 5, 5, 6, 7, 8, 9, 12

_____

5. 6, 3, 8, 7, 2

_____

6. 4, 2, 5, 6, 3, 10

_____

Tree Diagrams

Read carefully. Look at the diagram to answer the questions.

Probability helps us decide if something is likely or unlikely to happen. There can be many results to a problem. An outcome is a possible result. There may be one outcome or many. One way to find all the possible outcomes is to make a **tree diagram**. For example, look at the tree diagram below. This shows the possible outcomes of making a sandwich. To read a tree diagram, go from left to right. Follow each different line path to a different outcome. All the possible outcomes together are called a *sample space*.

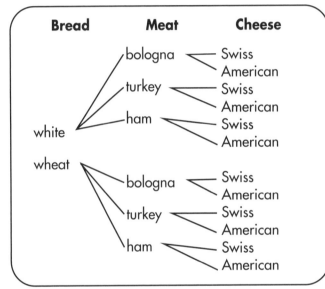

1. In probability, what is one possible result called?

    a. tree diagram

    b. sample space

    c. outcome

2. What is one way to find all possible outcomes?

    a. probability

    b. tree diagram

    c. draw lines

3. In the tree diagram above, how many possible outcomes are there? _____

4. Use the back of this paper to list all of the possible outcomes you found.

Survey Samples

Sometimes when you conduct a survey, you want to know the results of a group that is too large for you to ask everyone. So, you select a smaller group of people to survey.

The people you question are the **sample** of a larger group. It is important to find a sample that represents the larger group.

For example, suppose you want to know the favorite sport among students at your school. If you only ask members of the basketball team, they will likely answer basketball. A better sample would be all students in your class.

Does each sample described below fairly represent the larger group? Circle yes or no.

1. Larger group: third graders in your state   yes   no
    Sample: all third graders at Oakwood Elementary

2. Larger group: teachers from your school   yes   no
    Sample: every other teacher leaving a school
    assembly on Monday

3. Larger group: bus drivers in your school district   yes   no
    Sample: bus drivers at your school on a
    Wednesday afternoon

4. Larger group: elementary science students in Michigan   yes   no
    Sample: elementary students at a statewide
    science fair

Name _____

Prediction From a Sample

Geno conducted a survey about favorite sports in one third-grade class. The results of Geno's survey are in the table below.

Favorite Sports		
Sport	**Tally**	**Number**
baseball	卌	5
basketball	‖	2
biking			1
football	卌 卌	10
tennis	‖	2
volleyball			1

There are 8 third-grade classes in Geno's school. Each class has the same number of students.

1. Predict how many third graders in Geno's school favor basketball. _____

2. Predict how many third graders in Geno's school favor baseball. _____

3. Predict how many third graders in Geno's school favor tennis or volleyball. _____

4. Predict how many third graders in only 5 of the classes in Geno's school favor football. _____

Is It Likely?

What is the probability of the following events happening? Write one of the following words on each blank. Explain the reason for your choice.

> **Impossible:** would never happen
>
> **Unlikely:** does not have a very good chance of happening
>
> **Equally likely:** has the same chance as other options of happening
>
> **Likely:** has a good chance of happening
>
> **Certain:** will definitely happen

1. the probability you win the lottery tomorrow _____

2. the probability of having a driving license at 19 _____

3. the probability of the sun shining tomorrow _____

4. the probability Christmas will come in December _____

5. the probability you will need a hair cut in the next month _____

6. the probability of a clear sky tonight _____

7. the probability all students will be present in class tomorrow _____

8. the probability all students will be absent from class tomorrow _____

9. the probability you will wear red tomorrow _____

Name _____

Heads or Tails?

Follow the directions to conduct an experiment.

1. Get a coin to flip. Predict if it is more likely for the coin to land heads up or tails up, or if they are equally likely. Explain.

_____

2. Test your prediction. Flip the coin 20 times and record the results in the tally chart.

Result	Tally	Number
Heads		
Tails		

3. Did the experiment agree with your prediction? Explain why or why not.

_____

4. Repeat the experiment by flipping the coin 40 more times.

Result	Tally	Number
Heads		
Tails		

5. How did the results of your second experiment differ from your first experiment?

_____

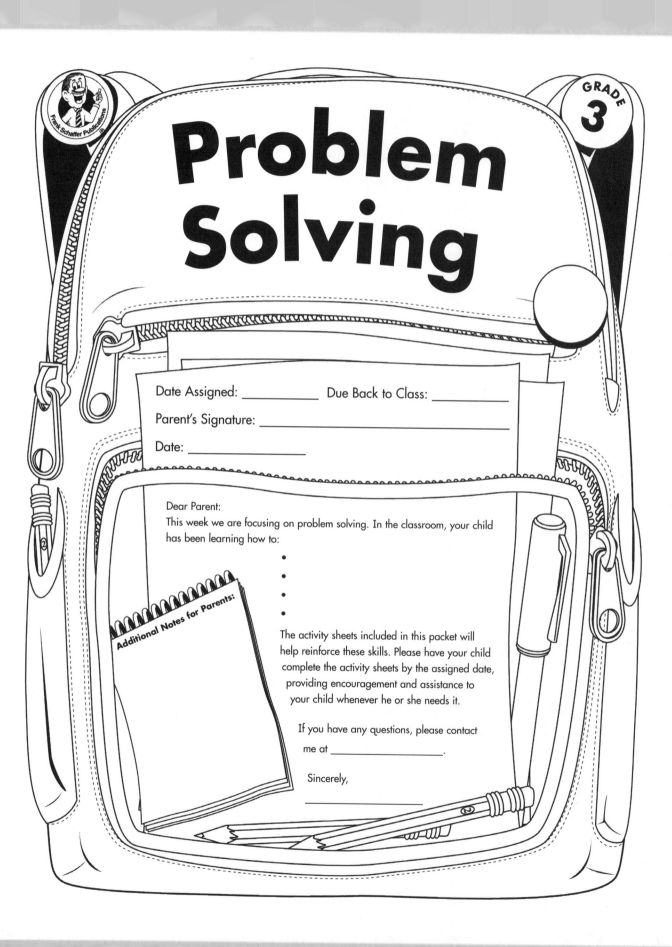

Problem Solving

GRADE 3

Date Assigned: _____ Due Back to Class: _____

Parent's Signature: _____

Date: _____

Additional Notes for Parents:

Dear Parent:

This week we are focusing on problem solving. In the classroom, your child has been learning how to:

-
-
-

The activity sheets included in this packet will help reinforce these skills. Please have your child complete the activity sheets by the assigned date, providing encouragement and assistance to your child whenever he or she needs it.

If you have any questions, please contact me at _____.

Sincerely,

_____

Name _____

Choose Your Operation

Read each problem. Circle the operation you would use to
solve it. You do not have to solve the problem.

+ − x ÷ **1.** 234 cars are in parking lot A. 289 cars are in parking lot B.
How many more cars are in lot B?

+ − x ÷ **2.** There are 7 squirrels in each of the 4 trees in our yard.
How many squirrels are in the yard?

+ − x ÷ **3.** 1,536 crayons were put into boxes of 24.
How many boxes were needed?

+ − x ÷ **4.** Ian earned $2.25 each time he watched his 2 sisters so his
mom could exercise. He watched them 23 times this month.
How much did he earn?

+ − x ÷ **5.** The container holds enough powder to make 32 quarts of a
drink. If each quart needs 4 scoops of powder, how many
scoops of powder are in the container?

+ − x ÷ **6.** Dan practiced piano 36 minutes on Monday, 42 minutes on
Tuesday, and 27 minutes on Wednesday.
How many total minutes did he practice?

+ − x ÷ **7.** Maddie has 22 children in her class. Her mom bought 176 small
snacks to put in bags. How many snacks go in each bag?

+ − x ÷ **8.** Luis bought a spool of fishing line that is 30 yards long. Each
yard is 3 feet long. How many feet of fishing line does he have?

Power Practice

Solve the problems on this page.

Opposites Assist

Solve. Check answers by using the opposite operation.

1. Yurelli counted 254 vowels on the first page in the book and 578 vowels on the second page. How many vowels in all?

2. 845 acorns were collected from one tree. 627 acorns were collected from another tree. How many more acorns were collected from the first tree?

3. Jade has $3.27 in her lunch account. The lunches she wants to buy this week will cost $5.25. How much money does she need to pay for her lunches?

4. Willie wants to watch one movie that is 78 minutes and another that is 120 minutes. How long will the two movies take?

5. Mikaela had 158 trading cards. She gave 39 to a friend. How many does she have left?

6. The scientists tagged 458 monarch butterflies the first week and 562 monarch butterflies the second week. How many butterflies were tagged during the two weeks?

Use Your Head

Estimate and solve the problem in your head. Write your answer. Then, solve using paper and pencil.

1. Gerard has a box of 24 crayons in his desk, a box of 16 crayons in his backpack, and a box of 64 crayons on his desk at home. He wonders if he has more than 100 crayons. Does he?

2. Hannah had 82 crickets in an aquarium. She fed 36 of them to her lizards. If no crickets die, does she have enough left to give the lizards 36 crickets next week?

3. Jeana wants to buy gum for 46 cents and a candy bar for 53 cents. She has 75 cents. Does she have enough money?

4. Elroy has two 64-ounce bottles of cola. He wants to fill a pitcher up to the line. It holds 150 ounces at that spot. Does he have enough cola?

5. Christopher needs 72 photo pockets in his album. He currently has 54 photos in them. He is bringing a roll of 24 to be developed. Will there be enough room for all 24 photos?

6. Maxine needs 80 cookies for school. She baked 36 with the first batch, 20 with the second batch, and 42 with the third batch. Does she need to make another batch of cookies?

Multiple Solutions

Mr. O'Donnel had a farm. On his farm, he had chickens and pigs and ducks and horses. The chickens and pigs liked to hang out in the pigpen. There are a total of 28 feet in the pigpen. How many chickens and pigs could there be?

1. Draw a picture to model one possible solution.

number of chickens = _____

number of pigs = _____

2. Should there be any "leftover" feet in this problem? Why or why not?

3. Reason with the numbers. Create a table of all possible solutions.

# of pigs								
# of chickens								

Riddles

Read the riddles to determine the coins. Use real coins or sketches to assist you.

1. I have 6 coins worth 28¢. The coins include 3 different kinds.
   What are the coins?

2. I have 9 coins worth 1 dollar. No coin is a nickel. What are the coins?

3. I have 3 different types of coins worth 96¢. The 18 coins include the same
   number of each coin. What are the coins?

4. My 4 coins total 80¢. No dime is in the bunch. What are the coins?

5. Not one of my 7 coins is a quarter. Their total value is 72¢. What are
   the coins?

6. Four types of coins combine to make my total value. My coins are worth 45¢.
   What are the coins?

7. My coins are worth 40¢. I have greater than 8 but fewer than 14 coins.
   What are the coins?

8. Show 2 ways to make 50¢. Choose one and write a riddle for it.

Use Your Math

Solve. Label your answer. Check your answers by making a picture or array, using repeated addition, using the inverse operation, or another strategy of your choice. Show your work.

1. Shelica has 4 packages of cookies. Each package has 60 cookies in it. How many cookies does she have in all?

2. Spencer completed 7 pages of homework. Each page had 8 problems. How many problems did he do?

3. Ellis has 36 action figures. Each box holds 6 figures. How many boxes does he need?

4. Nell received 12 letters a day for 6 days. How many letters did she receive?

5. Brenda had $36.00. She had just enough to purchase 3 math sets. How much did each set cost?

6. Theo's class was challenged to find as many 9-letter words as they could. Theo found 25. What is the total number of letters in his 25 words?

Name _____

Rocks in Space

Objects have different weights on the moon and the planets. Use the rules in the table to find the weight of these Earth rocks.

1. An object on the moon weighs about one-fifth of its Earth weight.
Divide by 5 to find the weights of each rock.

Pounds on Earth	10	20	25	35	50	55
Pounds on the Moon	2					

2. An object on Mars weighs about two-fifths of its Earth weight.
Follow the rules in the table to find the weight.

Pounds on Earth	50	45	40	30	25	10
a. Divide by 5	10					
b. Multiply by 2	20					

← Pounds on Mars

3. An object on Jupiter weighs about two and one-half times as much as it does on Earth.
Follow the rules in the table to find the weight.

Pounds on Earth	2	4	8	10	20
a. Multiply by 5	10				
b. Divide by 2	5				

← Pounds on Jupiter

4. Pretend you discover a planet where things weigh 3 times as much as on Earth.
Draw and fill in a table to show how the rates are related.

Power Practice

Math helps you study space science. Give an example of another science topic where math helps you.

Perimeter or Area?

Read each situation. Decide if the problem is asking about perimeter or area. Circle the appropriate answer choice.

1. Leo is putting up a fence around his garden.
How much fencing should he buy?   perimeter   area

2. Sara walks around her neighborhood block for exercise.
How far does she walk?   perimeter   area

3. Hector is painting his bedroom walls.
How much paint should he buy?   perimeter   area

4. Lou is putting wood trim around his dining room.
How much wood trim does he need?   perimeter   area

5. Dina is mowing her lawn.
How many square feet of grass does she cut?   perimeter   area

6. Mrs. Ling is sewing lace around the bedspread.
How much lace does she sew?   perimeter   area

7. The circus master puts a net under the trapeze acrobats.
How big is the net?   perimeter   area

Guess My Shape

1. I have 4 sides and 4 vertices. I have 4 lines of symmetry.
   You need only to measure one of my sides to find my perimeter.
   What shape am I? Draw me, and draw my lines of symmetry.

2. I have 4 equal sides and 4 vertices. I have 2 lines of symmetry, and
   I am not a square. What am I? Draw me, and draw my lines of symmetry.

3. I am around a lot. I have no sides. I have no angles either.
   What shape am I? Draw me. Label my parts.

4. I have more than 4 sides and fewer than 8. I have an even number of angles.
   What shape am I? Draw me.

Power Practice

Make up another riddle like these.

Name _____

Leap to a Conclusion

Use the line plot to answer each question.

3rd Graders' Long Jumps

```
                            X
                  X    X    X
             X    X    X    X
        X    X    X    X    X    X
   X    X    X    X    X    X    X    X    X
  24   25   26   27   28   29   30   31   32
```
Distance (inches)

1. Marcus claimed that more than half the class was able to jump at least 29 inches. Do you agree with his statement? Explain.

_____

_____

2. Courtney claimed that the range of the data is 7 inches. Do you agree with her statement? Explain.

_____

_____

3. A new student joined the class and jumped 29 inches. Will this jump affect the median, mode, or range. Explain.

_____

Answer Key

Place Value 10

Millions		Thousands						
2	9	5	1	0	6	3	8	4

1. 4   **2.** 3   **3.** 8   **4.** 9
5. 4   **6.** 8   **7.** 0

Valuation 11

1. 600   **2.** 10,000   **3.** 40
4. 400   **5.** 6   **6.** 20,000
7. 500,000   **8.** 10   **9.** 700
10. 20   **11.** 2,000   **12.** 0

Pull It Apart 12

1. 7,000 + 200 + 10 + 6
2. 30,000 + 4,000 + 900 + 20 + 8
3. 200,000 + 4,000 + 100 + 20 + 5
4. 800 + 30 + 1
5. 40,000 + 7,000 + 900 + 2
6. 600,000 + 10,000 + 6,000
7. 2,000 + 100 + 50 + 3
8. 90,000 + 300 + 6

Power Practice:

1. seven thousand, two hundred sixteen
2. thirty-four thousand, nine hundred twenty-eight
3. two hundred and four thousand, one hundred twenty-five
4. eight hundred thirty-one
5. forty-seven thousand, nine hundred two
6. six hundred sixteen thousand
7. two thousand, one hundred fifty-three
8. ninety thousand, three hundred six

Missing Information 13

1. representational form:

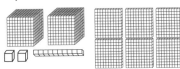

word form: given
standard form: 2,612
expanded form: 2,000 + 600 + 10 + 2; circle: even

2. representational form: given
word form: eight hundred forty-nine
standard form: 849
expanded form: 800 + 40 + 9; circle: odd

3. representational form

word form: three thousand, six hundred four
standard form: 3,604
expanded form: given; circle: even

4. representational form:

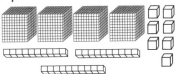

word form: four thousand, thirty-seven;
standard form: given;
expanded form: 4,000 + 30 + 7; circle: odd

Think About It 14

1. 5 tens   **2.** 24 tens
3. 8 tens   **4.** 50 tens
5. 127 tens   **6.** 5,679 tens
7. 3 hundreds   **8.** 20 hundreds
9. 89 hundreds   **10.** 9,214 hundreds
11. 520 hundreds   **12.** 1,200 hundreds
13. 9 thousands   **14.** 78 thousands
15. 510 thousands   **16.** 672 thousands
17. 30 thousands   **18.** 102 thousands
19. 1,250 tens, 125 hundreds
20. 390 tens, 39 hundreds
21. 4,000 tens, 400 hundreds, 40 thousands
22. 61,900 tens, 6,190 hundreds, 619 thousands

Comparisons 15

1. >   **2.** <   **3.** >   **4.** =   **5.** <
6. <   **7.** <   **8.** >   **9.** >   **10.** >
11. >   **12.** =   **13.** <   **14.** <   **15.** >
16. >   **17.** =   **18.** >   **19.** <   **20.** >

Answer Key

The Next Number Is 16
Wording of explanations will vary, example given.
1. 86, 96, 106
   explanation: ten is added to each number
2. 1238, 1236, 1234
   explanation: each number is reduced by 2
3. 300, 325, 350
   explanation: add 25 to each number
4. 960, 1070, 1180
   explanation: add 110 to each number
5. 69, 59, 49
   explanation: subtract 10 from each number

Power Practice: Students' answers will vary.

Odd or Even? 17
1. The sum of two even numbers is even.
2. The sum of two odd numbers is even.
3. The sum of an odd and an even number is odd.

Rounding 18
Tens

16→20	32→30	58→60
75→80	92→90	82→80
27→30	54→50	66→70

Hundreds

921→900	662→700	882→900
458→500	187→200	363→400
393→400	527→500	211→200

Thousands

2,495→2,000	3,379→3,000	4,289→4,000
7,001→7,000	8,821→9,000	6,213→6,000
5,111→5,000	9,339→9,000	2,985→3,000

Negative Numbers 19
1. −1   2. −4   3. −2
4. −3   5. +2   6. −1
7. −5   8. −6   9. +5

Fractions Among Things 21
1. 9   a. $\frac{2}{9}$ b. $\frac{4}{9}$ c. $\frac{3}{9}$
       d. $\frac{5}{9}$ e. $\frac{7}{9}$

2. 4   a. $\frac{1}{4}$ b. $\frac{2}{4}$ c. $\frac{1}{4}$
       d. $\frac{3}{4}$ e. $\frac{2}{4}$

3. 10   a. $\frac{1}{10}$ b. $\frac{2}{10}$ c. $\frac{4}{10}$
        d. $\frac{3}{10}$ e. $\frac{6}{10}$

4. 5;   a. $\frac{1}{5}$ b. $\frac{2}{5}$ c. $\frac{3}{5}$
        d. $\frac{4}{5}$ e. $\frac{5}{5}$

Fractions 22
1. $\frac{2}{4} = \frac{4}{8}$ 2. $\frac{1}{3} = \frac{2}{6}$ 3. $\frac{1}{3} = \frac{3}{9}$
4. $\frac{3}{4} = \frac{6}{8}$ 5. $\frac{1}{4} = \frac{3}{12}$ 6. $\frac{1}{2} = \frac{3}{6}$
7. $\frac{1}{3} = \frac{4}{12}$ 8. $\frac{1}{3} = \frac{5}{15}$ 9. $\frac{2}{3} = \frac{4}{6}$
10. $\frac{1}{2} = \frac{6}{12}$

More Fraction Practice 23
1. $\frac{2}{3} > \frac{1}{3}$ 2. $\frac{1}{4} < \frac{5}{8}$ 3. $\frac{3}{8} < \frac{2}{3}$
4. $\frac{3}{4} > \frac{1}{6}$ 5. $\frac{2}{7} < \frac{4}{7}$ 6. $\frac{2}{8} < \frac{1}{2}$
7. $\frac{4}{9} < \frac{2}{3}$ 8. $\frac{3}{6} > \frac{1}{4}$ 9. $\frac{3}{4} < \frac{4}{5}$

Get the Order 24
Groups should be shaded to reflect fractions given.

1. $\frac{1}{5}$ $\frac{2}{5}$ $\frac{3}{5}$ $\frac{4}{5}$ 2. $\frac{1}{8}$ $\frac{3}{8}$ $\frac{5}{8}$ $\frac{7}{8}$
3. $\frac{2}{6}$ $\frac{3}{6}$ $\frac{5}{6}$ $\frac{6}{6}$ 4. $\frac{0}{3}$ $\frac{1}{3}$ $\frac{2}{3}$ $\frac{3}{3}$
5. $\frac{2}{9}$ $\frac{4}{9}$ $\frac{5}{9}$ $\frac{6}{9}$ 6. $\frac{0}{4}$ $\frac{2}{4}$ $\frac{3}{4}$ $\frac{4}{4}$

Power Practice: You can place the fractions in order by their numerators when they have the same denominator.

Order the Parts 25
Circles should be shaded to reflect fractions given.

1. $\frac{1}{6}, \frac{1}{3}, \frac{1}{2}$ 2. $\frac{1}{12}, \frac{1}{8}, \frac{1}{4}$
3. $\frac{1}{12}, \frac{1}{5}, \frac{1}{2}$ 4. $\frac{1}{16}, \frac{1}{9}, \frac{1}{3}$
5. $\frac{1}{4}, \frac{1}{2}, \frac{1}{1}$

Answer Key

Tenths **26**
  1. 0.5   **2.** 0.8   **3.** 0.1
  4. 0.5   **5.** 3.2   **6.** 11.9
  7. 900.6   **8.** 0.2   **9.** 45.7
  10. 9.8   **11.** 18.5   **12.** 0.4
  13. 24.3   **14.** 120.3   **15.** 267.8
  16. 31.1
Power Practice: Grids should be shaded to reflect the following decimals: 0.3, 0.9, 0.6, and 0.2.

Hundredths **27**
  1. 0.09   **2.** 0.05   **3.** 0.01
  4. 0.07   **5.** 0.16   **6.** 0.89
  7. 0.45   **8.** 7.02   **9.** 5.04
  10. 16.11   **11.** 300.03   **12.** 709.04
  13. 612.71   **14.** 24.01   **15.** 33.02
Power Practice: Grids should be shaded to reflect the following decimals: 0.04, 0.09, 0.15, and 0.81.

Picturing Decimals **28**
  1. 50 small squares filled in or 5 columns
  2. 6 small squares filled in
  3. 61 small squares filled in or 6 columns and 1 square
  4. 34 small squares filled in or 3 columns and 4 squares
  5. 70 small squares filled in or 7 columns
  6. 4 small squares filled in
  7. 0.02   **8.** 0.6   **9.** 0.13
  10. 0.49   **11.** 0.08   **12.** 0.54

Dollars and Decimals **29**
  1. socks: $7; underwear: $10; shoes: $126; shorts: $27; jeans: $58; track suit: $69; shirts: $10, $16, and $29
  2. $7 + $10 + $126 + $27 + $58 + $69 + $10 + $16 + $29 = $352
  3. He will have approximately $8 left over. $360 − $352 = $8

Decimal Rounding **30**
  1. 0.3   **2.** 0.7   **3.** 0.2
  4. 1.6   **5.** 67.4   **6.** 21.1
  7. 3.6   **8.** 10.1   **9.** 93.0
  10. 451.95   **11.** 147.72   **12.** 5.20

  13. 17.18   **14.** 27.85   **15.** 36.66
  16. 231.16   **17.** 447.00   **18.** 52.58

Addition and Subtraction Families . . . **32**
  1. 8 + 9 = 17, 9 + 8 = 17, 17 − 8 = 9, 17 − 9 = 8
  2. 7 + 8 = 15, 8 + 7 = 15, 15 − 8 = 7, 15 − 7 = 8
  3. 15 + 19 = 34, 19 + 15 = 34, 34 − 15 = 19, 34 − 19 = 15
  4. 23 + 33 = 56, 33 + 23 = 56, 56 − 23 = 33, 56 − 33 = 23

Rebuilding the Pyramid **33**

1.
	97		
	48	49	
	25	23	26
14	11	12	14
6	8	3	9	5

2.
	59		
	28	31	
	12	16	15
3	9	7	8
0	3	6	1	7

3.
	49		
	23	26	
	10	13	13
4	6	7	6
2	2	4	3	3

4.
	78		
	38	40	
	18	20	20
9	9	11	9
5	4	5	6	3

5.
	96		
	45	51	
	20	25	26
9	11	14	12
4	5	6	8	4

6.
	97		
	50	47	
	27	23	24
14	13	10	14
5	9	4	6	8

Commutative Property of Addition . . . **34**
  1. 11, 11   **2.** 17, 17   **3.** no, no
  4. Answers will vary. Check student shading.
Power Practice: Students' answers will vary.

Associative Property of Addition **35**
  1. (4 + 5) + 9 = 4 + (5 + 9)
        9 + 9 = 4 + 14
          18 = 18
  2. (11 + 4) + 16 = 11 + (4 + 16)
        15 + 16 = 11 + 20
          31 = 31
  3. (5 + 8) + 12 = 5 + (8 + 12)
        13 + 12 = 5 + 20
          25 = 25
  4. (20 + 38) + 10 = 20 + (38 + 10)
        58 + 10 = 20 + 48
          68 = 68

Answer Key

Addition Practice 36

926	784	960	409	779
1,529	9,324	1,297	673	1,895
7,662	4,388	7,250	693	8,595
716	1,608	9,592	595	872
3,245	6,030	1,089		

Three-Digit Models 37
1. 518   **2.** 371   **3.** 187
4. 279   **5.** 98   **6.** 159

Subtraction 38
1. 266   **2.** 454   **3.** 397   **4.** 262
5. 394   **6.** 188   **7.** 491   **8.** 63
9. 273   **10.** 693   **11.** 281   **12.** 445

Using Estimation 39
1. 300 + 200 = 500, 528
2. 800 + 500 = 1,300, 1,235
3. 600 + 500 = 1,100, 1,081
4. 200 + 100 = 300, 344
5. 500 − 200 = 300, 234
6. 900 − 200 = 700, 716
7. 500 − 400 = 100, 152
8. 300 − 200 = 100, 153
9. 500 + 300 = 800, 754

Just Three Digits 40
1. largest = 931, smallest = 139
    139 + 931 = 1,070
    931 − 139 = 792
2. largest = 752, smallest = 257
    752 + 257 = 1,009
    752 − 257 = 495
3. largest = 831, smallest = 138
    831 + 138 = 969
    831 − 138 = 693
4. largest = 954, smallest = 459
    459 + 954 = 1,413
    954 − 459 = 495
5. largest = 875, smallest = 578
    578 + 875 = 1,453
    875 − 578 = 297
6. largest = 661, smallest = 166
    661 + 166 = 827
    661 − 166 = 495

Check With the Opposite 41
1. 620, 620 − 275 = 345
2. 521, 521 − 324 = 197
3. 506, 506 + 277 = 783
4. 314, 314 − 149 = 165
5. 539, 539 + 364 = 903
6. 136, 136 + 119 = 255
7. 254, 254 + 458 = 712
8. 480, 480 − 217 = 263
9. 251, 251 + 270 = 521
10. 1,439, 1,439 − 745 = 694
11. 679, 679 + 163 = 842
12. 538, 538 − 221 = 317

Groups 43
Each problem should include required sketch.
1. 12   **2.** 40   **3.** 30   **4.** 18
5. 36   **6.** 28   **7.** 24   **8.** 5
9. 45   **10.** 16   **11.** 42   **12.** 27

The Garden on the Balcony 44
1. 5 x 4 = 20   **2.** 7 x 6 = 42
3. 3 x 3 = 9   **4.** 5 x 10 = 50

Multiplication 45
1. 54   **2.** 15   **3.** 48   **4.** 18
5. 42   **6.** 30   **7.** 24   **8.** 72
9. 16   **10.** 24   **11.** 56   **12.** 28
13. 16   **14.** 25   **15.** 63   **16.** 27

Switching the Order 46
1. 21   **2.** 30   **3.** 6   **4.** 24
5. 18   **6.** 32   **7.** 14   **8.** 18
9. 36   **10.** 24   **11.** 10   **12.** 27

Answer Key

Zero and One Properties 47
1. Check student charts; zero property
2. Check student charts; identity property of multiplication
3. Check student charts; identity property of addition
4. Check student charts. The sums are 1 more, not the number you start with; the sums are not 0.
5. Check student charts.

Numbers in the Groups 48
1. 7 buttons per coat, $14 \div 2 = 7$
2. 8 flies on each window, $56 \div 7 = 8$
3. 4 spots on each bug, $36 \div 9 = 4$
4. 7 eggs in each nest, $35 \div 5 = 7$
5. 6 pretzels per bag, $42 \div 7 = 6$
6. 3 gems per ring, $18 \div 6 = 3$

Groups of Things 49
Each problem should include sketch.
1. 3   2. 2   3. 3   4. 3
5. 4   6. 5   7. 2   8. 3

Division 50
1. 4   2. 3   3. 7   4. 6   5. 4
6. 4   7. 2   8. 6   9. 9   10. 4

Related Operations 51
1. **a.–c.** Descriptions will vary. Students should mention properties or related operations.
2. **a.** $21 \div 3 = 7$
   b. $40 + 50 = 90$
   c. $17 \div 17 = 1$
   d. $29 - 29 = 0$

Multiplication and Division 52
1. 32   2. 35   3. 6   4. 9
5. 18   6. 6   7. 45   8. 28
9. 54   10. 4   11. 7   12. 24

Measure Me 54
1. 2.5 inches   2. 4 inches
3. 5.5 inches   4. 1 inch
5. 3 inches   6. 10 cm

7. 14 cm   8. 6 cm
9. 8 cm   10. 2 cm
pencil—18 centimeters   rubber eraser—2 inches
thumb tack—1 centimeter   paperclip—1.25 inches
tissue box—10 inches

Length Equations 55
1. $2 \times 12 = 24$, 24   2. $12 + 7 = 19$; 19
3. $30 \div 3 = 10$, 10   4. $3 \times 14 = 42$, 42
5. $(2 \times 36) + 20 = 92$, 92
6. $36 + (2 \times 12) = 60$, 60
7. $(3 \times 37) + 1 = 112$, 112
8. $(2 \times 36) + (2 \times 12) + 2 = 98$, 98
9. Answers will vary.

Metric Units of Length 56
1. 340 mm   2. yes   3. 300 cm
4. no   5. 5,000 m   6. 10 km

Perimeter 57
1. 12 cm   2. 36 in.   3. 89 ft.
4. 77 m   5. 65 km   6. 22 in.
7. 84 mm   8. 72 yds.   9. 33 m

Area 58
1. 10 square units   2. 6 square units
3. 6 square units   4. 9 square units
5. 9 square units   6. 7 square units
7. 10 square units   8. 8 square units
9. 5 square units   10. 11 square units
11. 11 square units   12. 8 square units

Shaded and Un-Shaded 59
1. 7 square units   2. 18 square units
3. 12 square units   4. 9 square units
5. 15 square units   6. 21 square units
7. 25 square units   8. 34 square units

Perimeter and Area 60
1. p = 12 units, a = 8 square units
2. p = 12 units, a = 9 square units
3. p = 26 units, a = 30 square units
4. p = 20 units, a = 24 square units
5. p = 20 units, a = 21 square units
6. p = 20 units, a = 16 square units
Power Practice: Students should indicate that the volume will remain the same.

Answer Key

Shape Designs. 61
Shapes will vary.

What Is Volume? 62
1. 5 cubes, 5 cubic units
2. 8 cubes, 8 cubic units
3. 9 cubes, 9 cubic units
4. 8 cubes, 8 cubic units
5. 10 cubes, 10 cubic units
6. 12 cubes, 12 cubic units

Prism Volume 63
1. 3 cubic units
2. 64 cubic units
3. 48 cubic units
4. 320 cubic units
5. 8 cubic units
6. 8 cubic units
7. 40 cubic units
8. 90 cubic units
9. 16 cubic units
10. 36 cubic units

Comparing Capacity 65
1. 6   2. 8   3. 8   4. 6   5. 16
6. 24   7. 6   8. 10   9. 2   10. 24

Metric Units of Capacity. 66
1. 2 L   2. 60 L   3. 3,000 L
4. 100 daL   5. 40 daL   6. .5 L
7. 2 kL   8. 5,000 L   9. 7 kL
10. 420 L   11. 4.5 kL   12. 90 L
13. 5 kL   14. 5 bottles

Selecting Appropriate Units 67
1. kL   2. kL   3. mL   4. L
5. mL   6. kL   7. mL   8. L
9. L   10. L   11. mL   12. L

Ounces and Pounds. 68
1. ounces   2. pounds
3. pounds   4. ounce
5. ounces   6–8. Drawings will vary.

Metric Units of Mass 69
1. 10,000 g   2. 10 dag   3. 2 kg
4. .5 kg   5. 7 t   6. 2,000 mg
7. 3,000 kg   8. 4.5 kg   9. 3 dag
10. 6 g   11. 40 kg   12. 5 hg
13. 10 stones   14. 35 cookies   15. 6 grams
16. 1,300 grams

Matching Clocks 70
1. b   2. d   3. c   4. e   5. a
6. j   7. f   8. i   9. h   10. g
Power Practice: 12:15, 12:45, 2:13, 3:45, 4:30, 5:00, 5:30, 9:20, 10:35, 11:45

Bathroom Countdown 71
1. 8:10   2. 7:06   3. 9:30
4. 4:59   5. 6:45

Temperature 72
1. 6°F   2. yes   3. 63°F
4. 28°F   5. 9°C   6. no

Show the Temperature 73
1. 20°F   2. 40°C   3. 32°F
4. 101°F   5. 0°C   6. 50°F

Using Money 74
1. $1.67;   2. $1.39
3. $1.36;   4. 2 and 3
5. quarters: 3, dimes: 9, nickels: 19
6. $1.46; needs 54¢; coins will vary for a total of 54¢.

Shapes in Line. 76
1. rectangle   2. star
3. big square; size
4. unshaded diamond; shading
Power Practice: Students' patterns will vary.

Which Way? 77
1. 15, growing; answers will vary
2. 93, 89; decreasing; answers will vary
3. 33, 29; decreasing; answers will vary
4. 118, 158; growing; answers will vary
5. 8, 64; growing; answers will vary
6. 104, decreasing; answers will vary
Power Practice: The pattern in problem 5 is different from the other patterns. This pattern increases by a different amount each time. The other patterns decrease or increase by a set amount.

Answer Key

Number Patterns **78**
1, 3, 5, **7**, **9**, 11, 13 (Rule +2)
70, **60**, 50, **40**, **30**, 20, 10 (Rule −10)
1, 8, 15, 22, **29**, **36**, **43** (Rule +7)
36, 33, 30, **27**, **24**, **21**, **18** (Rule −3)
115, 100, 85, **70**, **55**, **40**, **25** (Rule −15)
64, 55, 46, **37**, **28**, **19**, **10** (Rule −9)
17, 25, 33, **41**, **49**, **57**, **65** (Rule +8)
96, **90**, 84, 78, **72**, **66**, **60** (Rule −6)
88, **77**, 66, **55**, 44, **33**, **22** (Rule −11)
12, 24, 36, **48**, **60**, **72**, **84** (Rule +12)

Two-Step Pattern Rules **79**
  1. Students should write + 3 in the boxes above the pattern and − 2 in the boxes below the pattern.
  2. Add 3; then subtract 2.
  3. 10, 8, 11
  4. **a.** 26, 22, 29; add 7, subtract 4 (+ 7, − 4)
     b. 33, 34, 29; subtract 5, add 1 (− 5, + 1)
     c. 47, 42, 48; subtract 5, add 6 (− 5, + 6)
Power Practice: Students' patterns will vary.

Follow the Rule **80**
  1. **a.** 2, 3, 4, 5   **b.** 17, 15, 13, 11
     c. 5, 15, 25, 35   **d.** 1, 5, 9, 13
  2. **a.** 17, 20, 26, 62 **b.** 10, 4, 6, 39
     c. 0, 18, 22, 100 **d.** 9, 1, 3, 6
  3. **a.** IN: 10, 1; OUT: 12, 17
     b. IN: 2, 7; OUT: 24, 54

Guess the Rule **81**
  1. OUT: 7, 8, 11; Add 7
  2. OUT: 8, 7, 5; Divide by 3
  3. IN: 54; OUT: 15, 24; Subtract 9
  4. IN: 22, 42; OUT: 79; Subtract 21
  5. IN: 24, 8; OUT: 9; Divide by 4
  6. OUT: 28, 63; Multiply by 7
  7. IN: 3; OUT: 63, 90; Multiply by 9
  8. IN: 35, 7; OUT: 21; Add 11

Shape Values **82**
  1. **a.** 7   **b.** 12   **c.** 2
     d. 9   **e.** 30   **f.** 8
     g. 26   **h.** 13   **i.** 63

  2. 7; 7 + 5 = 12, 5 + 7 = 12, 12 − 5 = 7, 12 − 7 = 5
  3. 17; 12 + 5 = 17, 5 + 12 = 17; 17 − 12 = 5, 17 − 5 = 12
  4. 45; 9 x 5 = 45, 5 x 9 = 45, 45 ÷ 5 = 9, 45 ÷ 9 = 5
  5. No. Explanations will vary.

Number Letters **83**
  1. m = 26   **2.** a = 16   **3.** s = 58
  4. t = 38   **5.** u = 31   **6.** o = 19
  7. b = 20   **8.** f = 73   **9.** e = 40
  10. d = 52 **11.** r = 23 **12.** l = 22
  13. n = 42 **14.** g = 18 **15.** c = 17
Message: Number letters don't scare me!

Graphing Lines **84**
  1. Check student   **2.** Check student
    graphs; rectangle   graphs; triangle

Power Practice: Students should indicate that you need two points on a grid to make a line.

Name the Vertices **85**
  1. A (2, 6), B (7, 8), C (6, 2)
  2. S (8, 8), T (8, 3), U (2, 1)
  3. D (2, 4), E (2, 1), F (7, 1), G (7, 4), H (5, 7)
  4. L (2, 7), M (6, 7), N (9, 4), P (5, 4)
Power Practice: Answers will vary. Possible answer: counted right 5, and up 4

Parallel and Perpendicular Lines **87**
  1. perpendicular   **2.** neither
  3. neither   **4.** parallel
  5. parallel   **6.** perpendicular
Power Practice: parallel lines, perpendicular lines

The Right Angle **88**
  1. >   **2.** >   **3.** =   **4.** <
  5. =   **6.** <   **7.** <   **8.** >

Answer Key

Drawing Lines of Symmetry 89

1.
2.
3.
4.
5.
6.

Power Practice: Drawings will vary.

Match the Transformation 90

1.
2.
3.
4.
5.

Congruent or Similar? 91

1. similar   2. congruent   3. neither
4. similar   5. congruent   6. neither

Students will draw shapes to match in a size either smaller or larger than the one shown.

Types of Triangle 92

Types of Polygons 93

1. f. octagon   2. c. pentagon
3. a. triangle   4. b. quadrilateral
5. d. hexagon   6. b. quadrilateral
7. d. hexagon   8. g. not a polygon
                       (curved sides)
9. e. heptagon   10. g. not a polygon
                        (curved sides)

Cones, Cylinders, and Spheres 94

1. sphere or cylinder   2. sphere or cylinder
3. cylinder   4. cone   5. cylinder
6. cone   7. cone   8. sphere
9. cone   10. cylinder 11. sphere

How Many Faces and Edges? 95

1. 6, 12   2. 4, 6   3. 5, 8   4. 6, 12

What Will I Make? 96

1.
2.
3.
4.
5.
6.
7.
8.
9.
10.
11.

Make a Bar Graph 98

Graphs will vary. Sample graph is shown.

Answer Key

Circle Graph 99
1. 36
2. other board games
3. chess
4. same size
5. other board games
6. chess, other board games and checkers

Line Graph 100
1. how tall Carla was at each age
2. Go to 6 years old; then move up the graph to 44 inches.
3. Check student graphs.
4. a. about 53 inches
   b. about 42 inches
   c. uneven
   d. No, since the graph shows uneven growth, you cannot predict exactly.

Statistics 101
1. a. sum = 44; mean = 8.8 years
   b. median = 9 years
   c. No. Each number only occurs once.
2. a. mean = 4.8 miles
   b. median = 5 miles
   c. mode = 5 miles

The Range 102
1. 6   2. 6   3. 8
4. 7   5. 6   6. 8

Tree Diagrams 103
1. c
2. b
3. 12
4. white—bologna—Swiss
   white—bologna—American
   white—turkey—Swiss
   white—turkey—American
   white—ham—Swiss
   white—ham—American
   wheat—bologna—Swiss
   wheat—bologna—American
   wheat—turkey—Swiss
   wheat—turkey—American
   wheat—ham—Swiss
   wheat—ham—American

Survey Samples 104
1. no   2. yes   3. yes   4. no

Prediction From a Sample 105
1. 16   2. 40   3. 24   4. 50

Is It Likely? 106
1. unlikely   2. likely, if you live in the U.S.
3. Answers will vary, depending on time of year and weather forecast.   4. certain
5. Answers will vary.   6. Answers will vary, depending on time of year and weather forecast.
7. Answers will vary, but won't be certain or impossible.   8. Answers will vary.   9. Answers will vary.

Heads or Tails? 107
1. equally likely; Explanations will vary.
2. Experiments results will vary.
3. Results will vary.
4. Experiments results will vary.
5. Results will vary, but the more times this experiment is performed the more likely it is that the results will be 50% heads and 50% tails.

Choose Your Operation 109
1. −   2. x   3. ÷   4. x
5. x   6. +   7. ÷   8. x

Power Practice:
1. 55 cars   2. 28 squirrels
3. 64 boxes   4. $51.75
5. 128 scoops   6. 105 minutes
7. 8 snacks   8. 90 feet

Opposites Assist 110
1. 832 vowels, 832 − 254 = 578
2. 218 acorns, 218 + 627 = 845
3. $1.98, 1.98 + 3.27 = 5.25
4. 198 minutes, 198 − 120 = 78
5. 119 cards, 119 + 39 = 158
6. 1,020 butterflies, 1,020 −562 = 458

Answer Key

Use Your Head 111
1. Yes. He has 104 crayons.
2. Yes. She has 46 crickets left.
3. No. The gum and candy bar are 99 cents.
4. No. He has 128 ounces of cola.
5. No. He has 18 pockets left.
6. No. She has 98 cookies.

Multiple Solutions 112
1. Answers may vary. One possible solution is shown below.

(Chickens)   [pigs]

4 pigs and 6 chickens
2. There should not be any leftover feet. There can't be feet that are not attached to animals.
3.

# of pigs	0	1	2	3	4	5	6	7
# of chickens	14	12	10	8	6	4	2	0

Riddles 113
1. dime, dime, nickel, penny, penny, penny
2. 50-cent piece, quarter, dime, dime, 5 pennies
3. 6 dimes, 6 nickels, 6 pennies
4. 3 quarters, 1 nickel
5. 50-cent piece, 4 nickels, 2 pennies
6. 1 quarter, 1 dime, 1 nickel, 5 pennies
7. 1 quarter, 1 nickel, 10 pennies
8. Answers will vary.

Use Your Math 114
1. 240 cookies   2. 56 problems   3. 6 boxes
4. 72 letters   5. $12.00   6. 225 letters

Rocks in Space 115
1. 4, 5, 7, 10, 11
2. **a.** 9, 8, 6, 5, 2   **b.** 18, 16, 12, 10, 4
3. **a.** 20, 40, 50, 100   **b.** 10, 20, 25, 50
4. Table should show Earth weight in top row, Planet weight in second row. Numbers for Earth weight will vary. Planet weights should be 3 times as much.

Power Practice: Students' answers will vary.

Perimeter or Area? 116
1. perimeter   2. perimeter   3. area
4. perimeter   5. area   6. perimeter
7. area

Guess My Shape 117
1. square   2. rhombus   3. circle
4. hexagon

Power Practice: Students' answers will vary.

Leap to a Conclusion 118
Explanations will vary. Sample explanations are given.
1. yes; 12 out of 23 classmates jumped over 29 inches
2. no; 32 − 24 = 8
3. median; It will no longer be the middle data value.